SINGER

SEWING REFERENCE LIBRARY™

Sewing for the Home

Cy DeCosse Incorporated
Minnetonka, Minnesota

SINGER

SEWING REFERENCE LIBRARY™

Sewing for the Home

Contents

Also available from the publisher: *Sewing Essentials, Clothing Care & Repair, Sewing for Style, Sewing Specialty Fabrics, Sewing Activewear, The Perfect Fit, Timesaving Sewing.*

Library of Congress Cataloging
in Publication Data

Sewing for the Home

(Singer Sewing Reference Library)
Includes index.
1. Sewing 2. House Furnishings I. Series.
TT715.S48 1984   646.2'1   84-42638
ISBN 0-86573-203-5
ISBN 0-86573-204-3 (pbk.)

Distributed by: Contemporary Books, Inc.,
Chicago Illinois

CY DE COSSE INCORPORATED
Chairman: Cy DeCosse
President: James B. Maus
Executive Vice President: William B. Jones

SEWING FOR THE HOME
Created by: Cy DeCosse Incorporated, in
cooperation with the Singer Education
Department. SINGER is a trademark of
The Singer Company and is used under
license.

Project Director: Gail Devens
Production Director: Christine Watkins

Editorial Staff: Bernadette Baczynski, Paula Brewbaker, Christine Kittleson, Bernice Maehren
Art Directors: Nancy McDonough, William Nelson
Project Manager: Lucinda Hawker
Writers: Bernadette Baczynski, Betty Braden, Gail Devens, Judy Lindahl, Barbara Marhoeffer
Director of Photography: Buck Holzemer
Staff Photographers: Jim Brown, Tony Kubat, Jerry Robb

Production Staff: Michelle Alexander, Brian Berkey, Julie Churchill, Christopher Lentz, Douglas Meyers, Nancy Nardone, Jean Sherlock, Jennie Smith, Nik Wogstad
Consultants: Depth of Field Fabrics, Bruce Dixon, Zoe Graul, Zuelia Ann Hurt, Amy Long, Lynn Marquardt, Janet Schneider, The Singer Company, Carolyn Thurman, Waverly Decorative Fabrics
Sewing Staff: Phyllis Galbraith, Bridget Haugh, Julie Huber, Lynn Lohmann, Carol Neumann, Kathy Weber

Contributing Manufacturers: Coats & Clark, Inc.; Dyno Merchandise Corp.; Fairfield Processing Corp.; Marks International, Inc.; Risdon Corp.; The Singer Company

Color Separations: La Cromolito
Printing: R. R. Donnelley & Sons Co. (1287)

Fabrics from Waverly Decorative Fabrics, division of F. Schumacher & Company

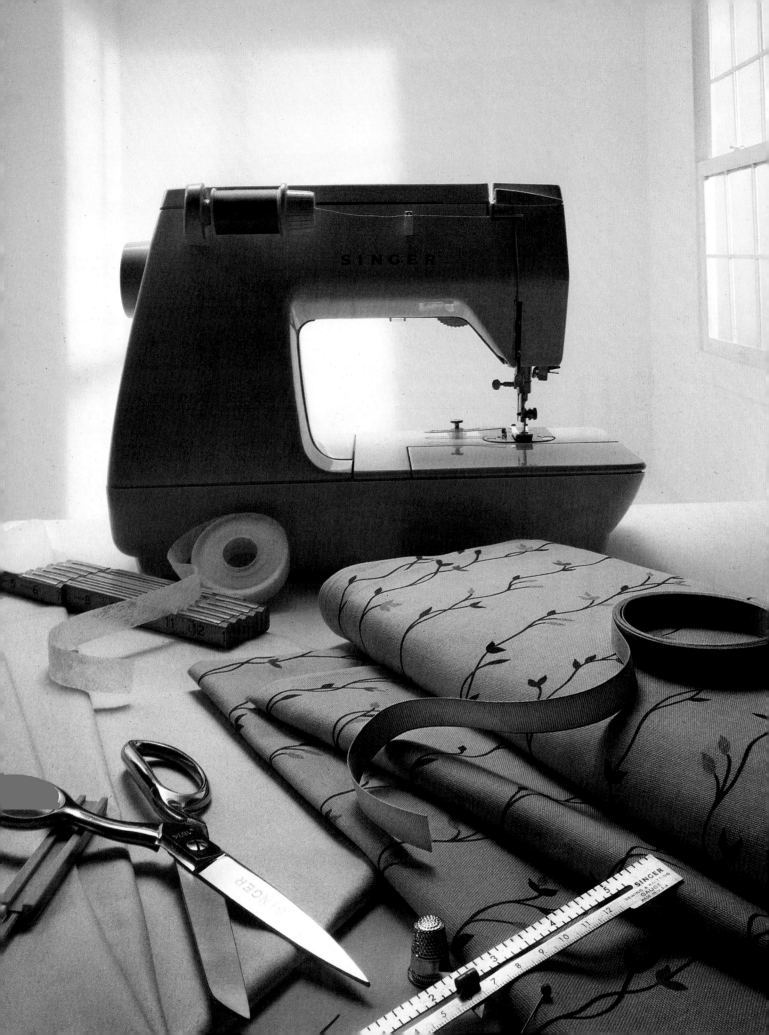

How to Use This Book

Sewing for the Home has a wide selection of decorator home fashions for you to sew. In making these items, we have considered cost, simplicity of construction, ease of care and coordination of colors and patterns. We have also considered the amount of time involved; many of these projects can be completed in an afternoon or evening. Also included, are designer customizing hints which you can incorporate into your home decorating projects.

Home Sewing Basics

We start with the basics of fabric and color selection, then show you how to use your sewing machine and its standard equipment to achieve the best sewing results. You will also learn about optional machine attachments that make home decorator sewing faster and easier.

Instructions for many of the projects include alternate sewing methods and suggest timesaving techniques such as fusible web to join two fabrics, fusible backing to stabilize a tieback, or hook and loop tape to close a pillow.

Before you begin to sew, read the information on pages 4 through 21 to acquaint yourself with the basic techniques of home decorator sewing.

Step-by-Step Guidance

This book is divided into four project sections: windows, pillows, tables and beds. For windows, we give instructions for standard favorites such as pinch-pleated draperies and ruffled curtains, along with directions for many other window fashions including five Roman shade variations. Pillows range from simple knife-edge styles to pillows with flanged or shirred edges. For tables, learn how to make a reversible tablecloth, quilted runners, bordered placemats and six different styles of napkins. Make a

bed comforter for your bed or cover an old one, then sew pillow shams and a dust ruffle to match.

At the beginning of each section is an overview of the section. This includes how to take accurate measurements for the projects and what to consider when selecting fabric and sewing aids. Cutting directions are detailed at the beginning of each project. For easy reference, fabrics and notions required to complete the project are included in boxes labeled YOU WILL NEED.

The step-by-step instructions that are given are complete; you do not need to purchase additional patterns. The photographs that accompany the instructions show you how the project should look at each step of its construction.

The sewing techniques you learn for one project can be applied to others. The same method is used for making ruffles on curtains as for pillows or bed accessories. The technique for mitering corners on a tablecloth is the same as on pillows or placemats.

Easy Home Decorator Projects

Experienced sewers can manage any of the projects we have designed; other projects such as knife-edge pillows, shower curtains, napkins or roller shades are suitable for less experienced sewers.

To inspire your creativity and help you visualize finished results, the projects throughout this book are made with coordinating fabrics. You will see how one fabric can be used for many different projects. Start with one project as the focal point of the room, then turn leftover fabrics from larger projects into attractive, coordinating accessories.

We hope the step-by-step guidance, practical shortcuts and designer tips given in *Sewing for the Home* encourage you to design and create your own home decorator fashions.

Fabrics for Home Decorating

Knowledge of fibers, finishes and fabrics will help you select the best fabrics for home sewing. Fiber and finish information is on the bolt-end label or printed on the selvage of decorator fabrics.

Terms to Know

Fiber is the basic unit of yarn before it is made into fabric. Fiber content affects durability and care.

Natural fibers come from nature. They are wool, cotton, silk and linen (flax). Natural fibers are durable, natural insulators.

Man-made fibers are chemically produced. Man-made fibers such as polyester, nylon and acrylic are usually associated with easy-care features and are well suited to home sewing projects.

Blends are combinations of fibers utilizing the best qualities of two or more fibers in one fabric.

A finish is a treatment to a fabric to change its behavior or improve its appearance, care or *hand* (how it feels). Finishes can make a fabric crease-resistant, mildew-resistant, resistant to oil or water-borne stains, or add luster and stability.

A permanent finish is often used to describe crease-resistance and shrinkage-resistance. Few finishes are truly permanent for the life of the fabric. Although they are durable, they may become less effective with laundering and dry cleaning.

Decorator fabrics are designed for home decorator projects. They are usually wider than 48" (122 cm) and often have special finishes which are desirable for home items.

Fashion fabrics are used primarily for dressmaker or fashion sewing, however, fabrics such as calico, eyelet, poplin, polished cotton, gingham, sateen and muslin may also be used for the home.

Repeat is the size (length and width) of the pattern or motif printed on the fabric. You will usually need to buy one extra repeat for each length of fabric you use. The size of the repeat is often printed on the label or selvage of decorator fabric.

Selvage is the finished lengthwise edge of a woven fabric.

Grain is the direction which fabric threads run. Woven fabrics consist of lengthwise threads intersecting crosswise threads. When these threads cross each other at perfect right angles the fabric is *on-grain*. If the intersection of lengthwise and crosswise threads is not at right angles the fabric is *off-grain*. Avoid buying fabric that is printed off-grain; it is difficult to work with and will not hang properly.

Other Practical Considerations

Fabrics should not be prewashed. Many are treated with finishes to protect their beauty and resist soiling. Washing may remove this finish, alter the fabric's hand, or fade the colors. Dry-clean your finished projects to keep them looking their best. If you do wash, use cold water and non-detergent soap.

Fabric Selection Guide

Project	Fabric suggestions	Appropriate finishes
Curtains, draperies	Lightweight sheer and semi-sheer fabrics: cotton, cotton-polyester blends, organdy, dotted Swiss, lace, batiste, voile. Mediumweight opaque fabrics such as textured and nubby cotton, linen and blends; open weaves; smooth surfaces such as chintz, polished cotton, antique satin, silk, moire.	Oil and water repellent; sunfast; mildew-resistant; preshrunk so that residual shrinkage will not exceed 1% in either direction.
Shades	For Roman shades and roller shades: closely woven fabrics such as sailcloth, denim, poplin, polished cotton. For bouffant shades: sheers and semi-sheers such as dotted Swiss, eyelet, cotton-polyester blends, chintz, polished cotton.	Oil and water repellent; sunfast; mildew-resistant; preshrunk so that residual shrinkage will not exceed 1% in either direction.
Linings, pillow liners	White or off-white sateen, muslin, sheeting.	Preshrunk linings for washable curtains and draperies.
Pillows, cushions	Closely woven fabrics to retain their shape, such as polished or textured cottons and linens, chintz, velveteen, corduroy.	Oil and water repellent; soil and stain-release.
Tablecloths, napkins placemats	Polished or textured cotton, linen, calico, cotton-polyester blends, quilted fabrics, loosely woven homespun-type cottons.	Oil and water repellent; soil and stain-release; colorfast; easy-care.
Comforters, covers, shams, dust ruffles	Closely-woven, washable fabrics: sheets, brushed cotton flannel, polished cotton, chintz. For ruffles: eyelet, dotted Swiss, lace.	Washable; colorfast; easy-care.

Mixing & Matching Fabrics

Using a number of complementary patterns and colors helps to connect areas in rooms and give your home continuity.

Geometric prints, stripes, patterns and solids can work together to give a room style and interest. Fabric manufacturers make it easy to coordinate fabrics by designing groups of complementary patterns, prints and solids which you can use in any combination.

If you coordinate fabrics on your own, unroll the bolts and compare them side-by-side in natural light. Examine the fabrics from several angles to judge the compatibility of print and color.

Bolts often come from different dye lots. To avoid problems of slight color variations or differences in pattern printing, buy fabrics for large projects from only one bolt. Check patterned fabrics to be sure they are printed on the straight grain. Also remember that wider fabrics generally mean fewer seams, especially in curtains.

Consider where the fabric will be used and how it relates to other fabrics in the room. Most stores have display cuts or swatch books of their decorator fabrics available. They may permit you to take swatches home. This gives you a chance to see the fabric next to other fabrics and lets you see it in your home lighting which may be very different from store lighting. If swatches are not available, ask for a sample from the bolt or buy a small piece before you invest in a large cut.

Choosing Colors

Keep these points in mind as you shop for fabrics.

• What colors already exist in the room? Take paint chips, carpet swatches or small cushions with you when you compare fabric.

• What wood tones are in your room? Fabric colors can enhance the natural tones and richness of wood.

• Color affects your mood. Pastels, neutrals and cooler shades, such as blues and some greens, are soothing. Bright shades and warmer colors like reds and yellows tend to stimulate. Dark colors create a cozy feeling.

• Color alters perceptions. Colors appear darker against light backgrounds, lighter against dark surfaces. Warm colors make objects seem larger, while cool colors make them recede. In general, avoid using bold contrasting colors in small rooms.

• Keep the room's exposure in mind. You may want to warm a northern exposure with warm tones, or cool down a hot sunny room with pale blues.

• Light colors show soil more readily than dark colors.

• At windows, pale colors diffuse light while dark colors block it. Hold up a length of fabric in direct sunlight to see if it creates the effect you want.

• Finally, consider your own preferences. Use these guidelines and your own taste to choose colors and patterns that beautify your home and reflect your personal style.

Equipment & Notions

The Basics

Home decorator sewing requires the same basic equipment as dressmaker sewing, with the addition of tools for measuring windows and furniture. Using the proper equipment makes the work easier and the results more satisfying.

1) Needle threader eases threading of hand and machine needles.

2) Pins with plastic or glass heads are easier to see and handle.

3) Thimble protects your middle finger when you sew by hand.

4) Needles for general hand sewing are *sharps*. Buy a package of assorted sizes for various sewing tasks.

5) T-pins are long, sturdy, broad-headed pins which are used to anchor fabrics to solid surfaces.

6) Quilting pins are extra long and useful for working with heavy or thick materials.

7) All-purpose thread is used for hand and machine sewing on most fabrics. Choose all-cotton, cotton-wrapped polyester or all-polyester thread, depending on the fiber content of the fabric.

Measuring Tools

The most important consideration in home decorator sewing is accurate measuring. The following measuring aids help you make correct calculations for buying and cutting fabric.

1) Carpenter's square is an L-shaped ruler, used to determine the perfect right angles and square corners that are essential to the fit of curtains, shades, tablecloths and pillows.

2) Wood folding ruler is used for measuring large areas. Because of its stability, this ruler is more accurate than a tape measure.

3) Yardstick is used for measuring long, flat lengths of fabric, and for marking and squaring grain lines. The surface of the yardstick should be smooth so it does not snag fabric.

4) Spring-return metal tape measures windows and other large areas. It is also handy for measuring around curves.

5) Seam gauge makes quick, short measurements such as those for hems. The 6" (15 cm) metal or plastic ruler has a sliding marker for accuracy in measuring.

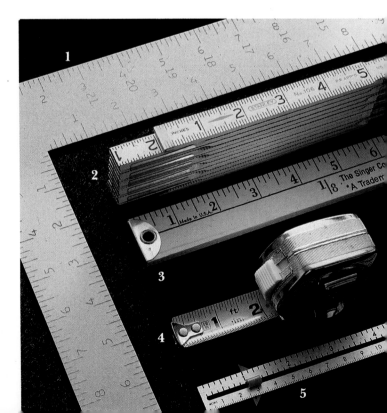

Marking & Cutting Tools

After making careful calculations and taking accurate measurements, mark and cut the fabric in preparation for sewing. Have on hand an assortment of marking tools for various fabric colors and textures. Good quality cutting tools are also a smart investment.

1) Cutting board is marked with horizontal and vertical lines, and is useful for laying out and cutting lengths of fabric up to 2 yards (1.85 meters). It is made of heavy cardboard so fabric can be pinned in place. Two boards may be necessary for large items such as floor-length curtains.

2) Tailor's chalk is specially designed to mark directly on fabric and rub off easily.

3) Trimmers have straight handles and are used for trimming and straightening edges. A lightweight, slim blade aids accuracy.

4) Seam ripper is used to remove stitches. Use it with care to avoid ripping fabric.

5) Bent-handled shears allow fabric to remain flat during cutting. Shears should be lightweight, easy to handle and 8" or 9" (20.5 or 23 cm) long.

6) Liquid marking pencils make sharp, defined lines on firm fabrics. One type of pencil makes a mark that can be removed with clear water; the other makes a mark that disappears in 48 hours. Test marking pencils on a fabric scrap before using. Ironing permanently sets the markings; if markings are on the right side of the fabric, do not press until they are removed.

Notions

Notions serve three purposes in home decorator sewing. Some, such as the rings used on Roman shades, are essential to the construction of an item; others, such as fusible web and fabric glue, make sewing easier. Notions such as braids, trims, pipings and ribbons are simply decorative.

1) Decorative trims such as bias tape (**1a**), piping (**1b**) and ribbon (**1c**) are available in a wide range of colors and styles to complement the items you sew. Select trims with the same care requirements as the decorator fabric.

2) Cords, tapes and rings (2a) have specific uses on certain projects. These notions are described in the directions for projects which require them.

3) Fusible web is used for hemming or for bonding two layers of fabric together. It is available in narrow strips for hems, or in 18" (46 cm) widths for fusing larger areas.

4) Fabric adhesives such as glue stick (**4a**) and craft or white glue (**4b**) may be used for temporary basting, or for permanently applying batting or trims to items which will not receive much handling.

5) Liquid fray preventer dries invisibly and prevents the raw edge of fabric from fraying. Use it as a temporary agent to prevent raveling while working with fabric, or as a permanent finish on exposed seams and edges.

6) Stain-resistant spray can be used on many home decorating items to prevent spills from soaking into fabric. To apply, follow instructions on the container.

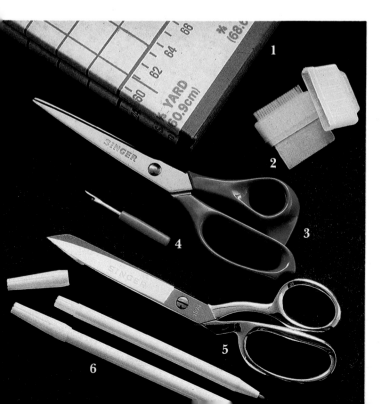

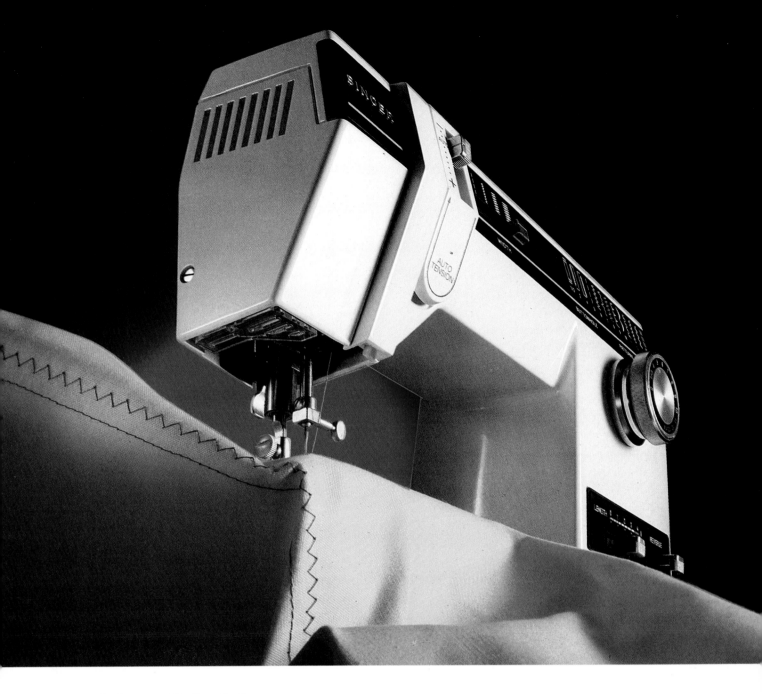

Machine Stitching

Most home decorator sewing can be done entirely by machine with a straight or zigzag stitch. Although machines vary in capabilities, each has the same basic parts and controls. Consult your machine manual to review the threading procedures and to locate the controls that operate the principal parts.

Tension, pressure and stitch length are the three main adjustments that create perfect straight or zigzag stitching. Choosing the appropriate needle and thread for the sewing project and fabric also helps to create quality stitching.

Tension is the balance between the upper and bobbin threads as they pass through the machine.

When tension is perfectly balanced, the stitches look even on both sides of the fabric because they link midway between fabric layers. Tension that is too tight causes seams to pucker and stitches to break easily. Tension that is too loose results in weak seams with stitch links on the bottom layer of fabric.

Pressure regulates the even feeding of fabric layers. When pressure is too heavy, the bottom fabric layer gathers, forcing the upper layer ahead of the presser foot. This unevenness can make a difference of several inches at the end of a long seam, such as one on a curtain. Pressure that is too light may cause skipped stitches, crooked stitching lines and weak, loose stitches.

Stitch length is controlled with a regulator that is on an inch scale from 0 to 20, a metric scale from 0 to 4, or a numerical scale from 0 to 9. On the metric and numerical scales, higher numbers form a longer stitch, lower numbers a shorter stitch. For normal stitching, set the regulator at 10 to 12 stitches per inch (2.5 cm). This setting is equivalent to 2.5 to 3 on the metric scale, and 5 on the numerical scale.

Needle, size 14/80, is used for general-purpose sewing on mediumweight fabrics. Because the firm weave and glazed finish of many home decorator fabrics dull a needle quickly, change the needle often. A bent, blunt or burred needle damages fabric. Avoid damage to the needle by removing pins from the seam as you come to them. Never sew over pins or let them get under the fabric where they may come in contact with the feed.

Thread for general-purpose sewing is suitable for most home decorator projects. Use an all-purpose weight. Choose all-cotton, all-polyester, or cotton-wrapped polyester thread that matches the fiber content of the fabric. For balanced tension, use the same type of thread in the bobbin and the needle.

Thread the machine correctly; incorrect threading can cause a problem stitch. To rethread the machine, remove the spool completely and begin again, in case the thread has tangled in the tension or over the spindle.

Use a scrap of fabric to test the tension, pressure and stitch length before starting to sew. To check the balance of the tension, thread the machine with different colors for upper and bobbin threads so the stitches are easier to see.

Perfect Straight & Zigzag Stitching

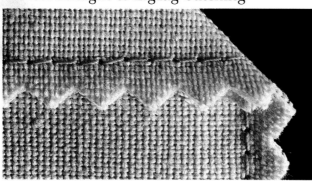

Straight stitches should link midway between fabric layers so stitches are the same length on both sides of fabric. Adjust tension and pressure so stitches do not break easily and the seam does not pucker.

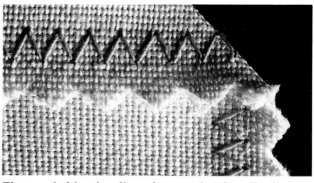

Zigzag stitching is adjusted correctly when the links interlock at the corner of each stitch. Stitches should lie flat. Adjust the zigzag width and density with the stitch length and width regulators.

Machine Stitching Terms

Bastestitching (a) is the longest straight stitch on the machine: 6 on the inch scale, 4 on the metric scale, and 9 on the numerical scale. Some sewing machines have a separate built-in bastestitch **(b)** that makes two stitches to the inch (2.5 cm). Use it for speed-basting straight seams.

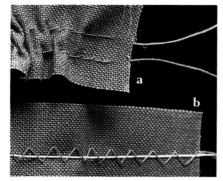

Gathering stitch is done with two rows of bastestitching placed ½" (1.3 cm) and ¼" (6 mm) from the fabric edge. Loosen tension, use heavier bobbin thread, and pull up bobbin thread to form gathers **(a)**. For long areas of gathers, zigzag over cord, string or dental floss without catching cord in the stitch **(b)**. Pull up cord to gather.

Edgestitching is placed on the edge of a hem or fold. The straight-stitch foot and straight-stitch plate aid in the close control needed for this stitching. The narrow foot rides on the folded edge, and the plate's small needle hole keeps fragile fabric from being drawn into the feed.

Basic Seams

All seams in home decorator sewing are ½" (1.3 cm) unless otherwise specified. To secure straight seams, backstitch at each end of the seam by stitching in reverse for ½" (1.3 cm). Four seam techniques are used in home decorator sewing.

1) Plain seam is suitable for almost every fabric and sewing application when you plan to enclose the seam or cover it with a lining.

2) French seam eliminates raw edges in exposed seams. In dressmaking, the French seam is used primarily on sheer fabrics; in home decorating use it whenever a seam is visible on the wrong side or is subjected to frequent laundering.

3) Interlocking fell or self-bound seam, like the French seam, completely encloses raw edges. For this seam, sew on the wrong side of the fabric. Use the narrow hemmer attachment as a timesaver.

4) Overedge or zigzag seams are plain seams with a zigzag finish to prevent raveling. Use them on heavy, textured fabrics that are too bulky for French or self-bound seams. Some machines have overedge settings that stitch and finish the edge in one step. For this seam, allow ¼" (6 mm) seam allowances.

Long straight seams tend to pucker in some fabrics, especially sheers. To prevent this, practice taut sewing. As you sew, pull equally on the fabric in front and back of the needle as if the fabric were in an embroidery hoop. Do not stretch. Pull the fabric taut, and let it feed through the machine on its own.

How to Sew a Plain Seam

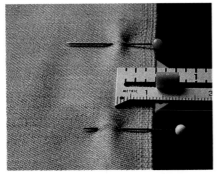

1) Pin right sides of fabric together, with pins on seam line at right angles to raw edge for easy removal. If using basting tape, place it on the raw edge to prevent stitching through it.

2) Use seam guide to sew even seams. Backstitch to secure; then stitch seam, removing pins as you come to them. Backstitch at end of seam. Lift presser foot and remove fabric by pulling 2" to 3" (5 to 7.5 cm) of thread to the left.

3) Clip threads close to the end of seam. Press seam open or to one side. If seam is on the selvage, clip diagonally into selvage every 1" (2.5 cm) to prevent puckering.

How to Sew a French Seam

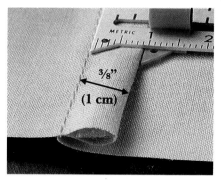

1) Pin *wrong* sides of fabric together. Stitch a scant ¼" (6 mm) seam. Press seam allowance to one side. For narrower finished seam, trim seam allowance to ⅛" (3 mm).

2) Turn fabric panels right sides together to enclose the trimmed seam allowance. Stitching line should be exactly on fold.

3) Stitch ⅜" (1 cm) from folded edge, enclosing first seam. Press the seam to one side. If first seam was trimmed, stitch ¼" (6 mm) from the edge.

How to Sew an Interlocking Fell Seam

1) Pin fabric, right sides together, with edge of top layer ½" (1.3 cm) from edge of bottom layer. Stitch ¾" (2 cm) from edge of bottom fabric layer.

2) Fold and press ¼" (6 mm) on seam allowance of bottom layer so that it meets edge of top layer. Fold and press again, covering the stitching line.

3) Edgestitch close to fold. Press seam to one side, gently pulling it straight to eliminate puckering. Or use narrow hemmer for final stitching (page 18).

Three Ways to Sew an Overedge Seam

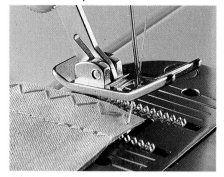

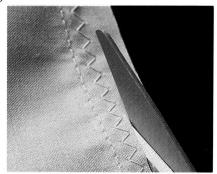

Zigzag plain seam. Stitch ½" (1.3 cm) plain seam. Zigzag seam allowances together close to raw edge. This eliminates trimming the seam, but results in a wider seam. Press seam to one side. This is the easiest overedge seam to sew and is suitable for most fabrics.

Zigzag narrow seam. Stitch ½" (1.3 cm) plain seam. Zigzag seam allowances together, stitching with wide zigzag close to stitching. Trim seam allowances close to zigzag stitching. This seam requires time for trimming. Use it as an alternative to French seams.

Overedge seam. Trim seams to ¼" (6 mm) before stitching. Then stitch seam with built-in overedge stitch. This makes a straight seam and zigzags over cut edge in one step. Use this seam on medium to heavyweight fabrics which ravel.

Timesaving Accessories

Many home decorator sewing projects require long seams or hems. There are several machine attachments and special feet that speed hemming, binding, ruffling and straight stitching. Some of these accessories come with the machine; others are available from your machine dealer.

Before buying special-purpose attachments, find out if your machine has a high, low or slanted shank. Consult the machine manual if you are not sure what type of shank your machine has. Snap-on presser feet will fit any machine with a snap-on, all-purpose shank.

Special-purpose foot is used for decorative stitching and machine embroidery. The plastic foot lets you see the stitching easily, and a groove under the foot allows for a build-up of thread. Use the foot for general-purpose sewing and special tasks such as closely-spaced zigzag overedge.

Zipper and cording foot is used for inserting zippers, applying snap tape and for making and applying cording. It adjusts to either side of the needle, allowing stitching to be placed close to bulk on one side of the seam.

Even Feed™ foot feeds top and bottom layers of fabric at the same rate, ensuring that seams start and end evenly. This foot helps keep plaids and other matched designs aligned in long seams. Use on heavy, bulky or quilted fabrics, as with insulated shades.

Narrow hemmer automatically double-folds the fabric edge and stitches a ⅛" (3 mm) hem without pressing or pinning. The foot is useful for hemming and for stitching interlocking fell seams.

Seam guide helps keep seam allowances even. It attaches to the bed of the machine (a) and adjusts for seam widths up to 1¼" (3.2 cm). A magnetic seam guide (b) attaches to any metal machine bed.

Quilter guide-bar rides in the first row of stitching to form perfectly parallel quilting lines. Use it for topstitching or channel quilting. The bar adjusts to widths up to 3" (7.5 cm) and can be used on either side of the needle.

Ruffler Attachment

Ruffler attachment automatically gathers strips of light or mediumweight fabric. Stitch length affects fullness; short stitches give more fullness and longer stitches give less. Gather one layer of fabric **(a)**.

Or gather one layer and attach it to another layer of fabric in one step **(b)**. Insert fullness at every stitch, or at 6 or 12-stitch intervals. Use this attachment for ruffles on curtains, pillows or dust ruffles.

Blindstitch Hem Foot & Guide

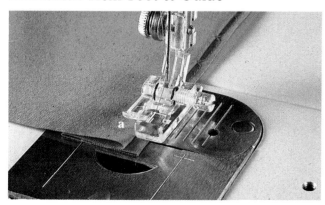

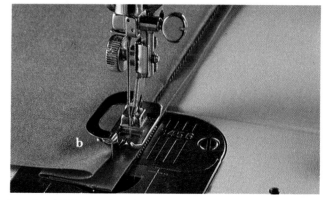

Blindstitch hem foot is used with the built-in blind hemming stitch. The foot **(a)** positions the hem for sewing with straight and zigzag stitches which are

barely visible on the right side. Blindstitch hem guide **(b)** is used with the general-purpose foot to position the hem for blindstitching.

Binder Attachment

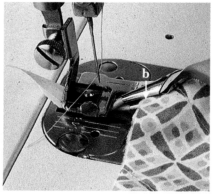

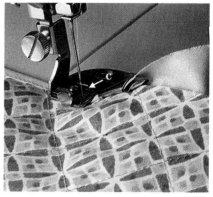

Binder attachment is used to fold and attach bias bindings in one step. First, cut a sharp point at end of bias strip. Feed point through scroll on foot **(a)**. Pull point through

so strip folds to the inside. Sew a few stitches to hold bias fold in place. Insert fabric to be bound into slot between scroll edges **(b)**. Adjust position of foot so that

needle stitches on edge of fold **(c)**. Guide fabric gently as you stitch. Use the binder attachment for finishing edges of any fabric.

Hand Stitching

Almost all sewing for home decorator projects can be done on the machine, but sometimes hand stitching is necessary. Closing seam openings on pillows, attaching trims and finishing hems are tasks which may require delicate hand sewing.

To make hand stitching easier, run the thread through beeswax to make it stronger and prevent it from snarling. Use a long needle for the running stitch. Hemming and tacking are usually easier with a short needle.

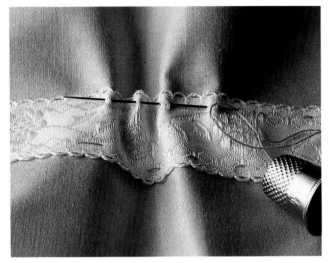

Running stitch is a straight stitch used for temporary basting, easing, gathering or stitching seams. Work from right to left, taking several stitches onto needle before pulling it through. For easing or gathering or for seams, make stitches ⅛" to ¼" (3 to 6 mm) long. For basting, make stitches ½" to ¾" (1.3 to 2 cm) long; use longer stitches for speed-basting.

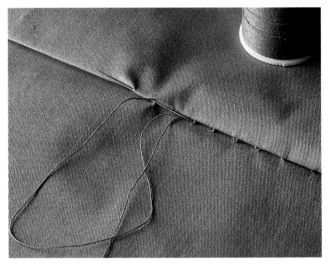

Slipstitch is a nearly invisible stitch for hems, seam openings, linings or trims. Work from right to left, holding folded edge in left hand. Bring needle up through fold and pull thread through. Then take a tiny stitch in body of fabric, directly opposite point where thread came out. Continue taking stitches every ¼" (6 mm).

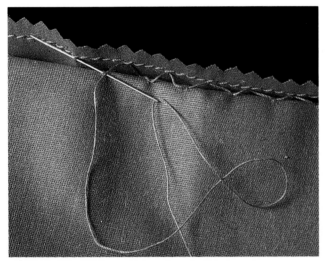

Blindstitch makes a hem that is inconspicuous from either side. Work from right to left with needle pointing left. Take a tiny stitch in body of fabric. Roll hem edge back slightly and take next stitch in underside of hem, ¼" to ½" (6 mm to 1.3 cm) to left of first stitch. Do not pull thread too tightly.

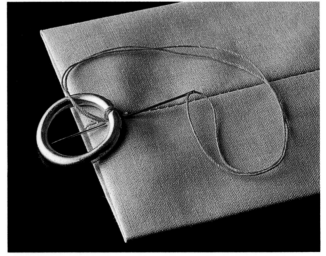

Tacking is used to attach rings and weights, secure linings or hold facings in place. Using double thread, take two or three stitches in the same place, one on top of the other. Secure with a backstitch. When tacking through more than one layer of fabric, do not sew through to outside layer.

Padded Work Surface

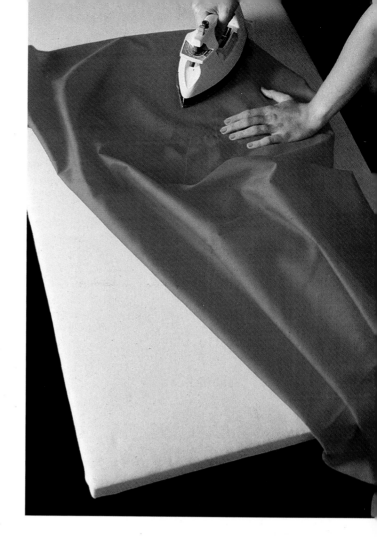

Make a padded work surface to lay out an entire panel for cutting, measuring, squaring off ends and pressing. The square corners and ample width make it easier to work with square and rectangular shapes. Fabric does not slide on the muslin-covered surface; you can also pin into it and press directly on it.

For small projects, use the *square* end of a regular ironing board as a work surface.

Use a steam-spray iron for all your pressing needs. To press fabric, lift and lower the iron in one place. This up-and-down motion prevents fabrics from stretching or distorting. Let the steam do the work. To make sharp creases or to smooth a stubborn wrinkle, spray the fabric with water or spray sizing.

YOU WILL NEED

Hollow door or ¾" (2 cm) plywood, approximately 3' × 7' (.95 × 2.16 m), set on saw horses.

Padding, cotton batting (not polyester), table pads or blankets, ¼" to ½" (6 mm to 1.3 cm) thick, enough to overlap door or plywood 6" (15 cm) on all sides.

Muslin or unpatterned sheet, approximately 6" (15 cm) larger than door or plywood on all sides.

How to Make a Padded Work Surface

6"
(15 cm)

1) Place layers of padding on the floor or on a large, flat surface. Center the door on top of the padding; cut padding 6" (15 cm) larger than the door on all sides.

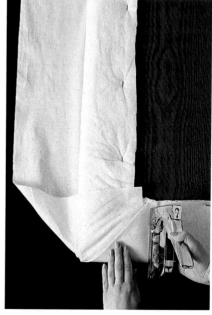

2) Fold padding over one long edge of the door and tack with 4 or 5 staples. Pull padding on opposite edge and tack. Repeat on both ends. Secure with staples 3" (7.5 cm) apart.

3) Center padded door on top of muslin. Wrap and fasten with staples 3" (7.5 cm) apart. Turn right side up and spray muslin with water. As it dries, muslin shrinks slightly so cover fits tightly.

Curtains

Curtains are a traditional favorite for window fashions. They are flat, non-pleated panels, so they are easier to clean and press than many other window treatments.

Curtains are often made of lightweight or sheer fabrics. Heavier fabrics such as linen, chintz, or textured or polished cotton look best for formal, floor-length curtains. Lighter, crisper fabrics work well for casual, sill-length and cafe curtains. Sheer curtains are usually two and one-half to three times the fullness of the finished width; heavier fabrics require only double fullness.

Mount curtains at windows on stationary rods or poles. Rods may be plain, covered with shirred fabric between the curtain panels, or wide and flat such as Continental™ and cornice rods.

Casings, also known as rod pockets, are hems stitched in place along the upper edge of curtains. The hems are open at both ends so a curtain rod or pole can be inserted.

Headings are optional on curtains. The heading is a decorative ruffle above the casing along the curtain's upper edge.

Linings add weight and body to curtains. Although a lining may not be necessary, it can improve a curtain's appearance and give it a custom look.

Tab top curtains have fabric loops instead of a casing along the curtain's upper edge. These curtains are used with decorative brass or wooden poles.

Ruffled curtains have a graceful appearance. Ruffles add weight to curtains and make them hang and drape more attractively.

Tiebacks are separate fabric strips which hold curtains open and emphasize the drape of the curtain. Tiebacks can be straight, shaped or ruffled and are usually stationary on panel curtains.

Shower curtains are flat, one-piece, hemmed curtains with evenly-spaced holes along the upper edge for hanging.

Casing Styles for Curtains

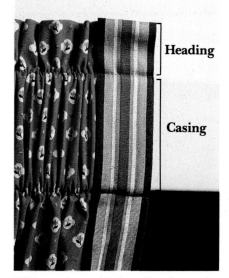

Simple casing is stitched along the upper edge of the curtain. Simple casings are used for sheer curtains which hang behind draperies, a valance or cornice.

Casing with heading. Headings create a ruffled edge above casings. Headings are from 1" to 5" (2.5 to 12.5 cm) deep, depending upon curtain length and weight of the fabric.

Wide casing with heading is used with a Continental or cornice rod. It is well suited for curtains on tall windows or floor-length curtains, where heading depth should balance with curtain length.

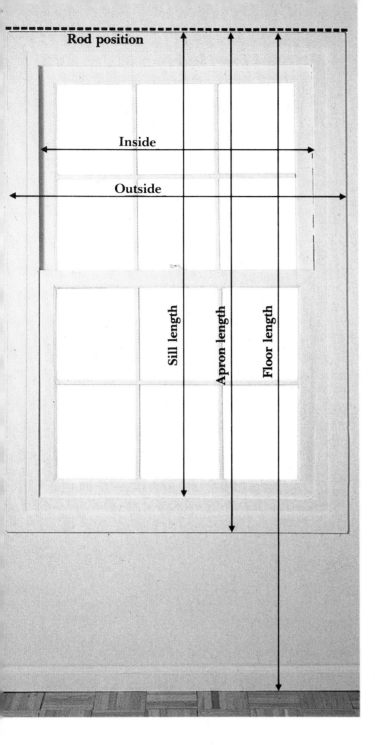

Rod position

Inside

Outside

Sill length

Apron length

Floor length

Measuring the Window

Before measuring windows, select the style of curtain, drapery or shade you will make. The style of window treatment determines what installation hardware is necessary. Next, decide exactly where the window treatment will be placed; install the hardware and measure this area for the finished size of the curtain, shade or drapery.

Curtain rods may be attached to the window frame, within or at the sides of the frame, on the wall above the frame, or at the ceiling.

Mounting boards are necessary for hanging Roman shades and other shades based on the Roman shade construction. These 1" × 2" (2.5 × 5cm) boards are cut to the width of the shade, stapled or tacked to the shade's upper edge, then installed at the window. An *inside mounted* shade fits firmly inside the top of the window frame. An *outside mounted* shade is installed on the wall above the frame. A *hybrid mounted* shade is a combination mount. The mounting board is placed inside the window, but the shade is the width of the outside mount.

Roller shades are installed inside or on the window frame, or on the wall above.

Follow these guidelines for accurate measuring:

1) Use a folding ruler or metal tape for measuring; cloth tapes may stretch or sag.

2) Measure and record the measurements for all windows separately, even if they *appear* to be the same size. Size differences, even if slight, should be taken into account when constructing window treatments.

3) When measuring for a shade that fits inside the window, measure the window width at the top, center and bottom to determine if it is true and square.

4) When measuring for curtains on a window without an apron, measure to at least 4" (10 cm) below the sill.

Window Measurements for Curtains, Shades and Draperies

Treatment	Finished Length	Finished Width
Curtains	Measure from top of rod or heading to desired length (sill, apron or floor).	Measure rod from end to end, including *returns* (short ends of rod which stand out from wall).
Roller Shades	Measure from top of roller to sill.	Measure length of roller.
Other Shades	Measure from top of mounting board to sill or desired length.	Measure mounting board from end to end.
Shower Curtain	Measure from bottom of rod to desired length.	Measure length of rod.
Use these measurements with chart (page 27) to estimate amount of fabric needed.		

Estimating Yardage

Because fabric widths vary, yardage cannot be figured until the fabric has been selected. After you have taken the necessary measurements and determined the finished size of the curtain, shade or drapery, you must add to the length and width for seams, hems, headings and fullness. This is the *cut length*. Use the cut length to estimate the amount of fabric you will need. For curtains and draperies, use the amounts as listed below and transfer the correct amount to the chart, (right). For shade yardage, see individual instructions for each type of shade.

Determining Length

To the *finished length*, add the amount needed for lower hems, casings, headings and pattern repeat.

Lower hems. For mediumweight fabrics, use a 3" (7.5 cm) hem; add 3½" (9 cm) to the length. For sheer and lightweight fabrics, use a double-fold hem of 2" to 3" (5 to 7.5 cm); add 4" to 6" (10 to 15 cm) to the length. A deeper hem of 5" to 6" (12.5 to 15 cm) can also be used; allow double the amount for length.

Casings/headings. For simple casings with no heading, add an amount equal to the diameter of the rod plus ½" (1.3 cm) to turn under and ¼" to 1" (6 mm to 2.5 cm) ease. The amount of ease depends on the size of the rod and thickness of the fabric. Lightweight fabrics require less ease; casings for large rods require more. For casings with headings, use the formula for a simple casing, adding to it an amount twice the depth of the heading.

Pattern repeat. Fabrics with patterns (motifs) need to be matched. Measure the distance between motifs and add that amount to the length of each panel.

Determining Width

To the *finished width*, add the amount needed for seams, side hems and fullness.

Seams. For multi-width panels, add 1" (2.5 cm) for each seam. Panels which are not wider than the fabric do not require an extra amount for seams.

Side hems. Add 4" (10 cm) per panel for a 1" (2.5 cm) double-fold hem on each side of the panel.

Fullness. Fabric weight determines fullness. For medium to heavyweight fabrics, add two to two and one-half times the finished width of the curtain. For sheer and lightweight fabrics, add two and one-half to three times the finished width.

Make a copy of this chart and fill it in to help you figure the correct amount of fabric needed for curtains, shades or draperies.

Yardage Estimation

Cut Length	in. (cm)
For fabrics *not* requiring pattern match:	
1) Finished length	
2) Bottom hem (double for most fabrics)	+
3) Casing/heading	+
4) Cut length for each width or part width	=
For fabrics requiring pattern match:	
1) Cut length (figure as above)	
2) Size of pattern repeat (distance between motifs)	÷
3) Number of repeats needed*	=
4) Cut length for each width or part width: multiply size of repeat by number of repeats needed	

Cut Width	
1) Finished width	
2) Fullness (how many times the finished width)	×
3) Width times fullness	=
4) Side hems	+
5) Total width needed	=
6) Width of fabric	
7) Number of fabric widths: total width needed divided by width of fabric*	

Total Fabric Needed	
1) Cut length (as figured above)	
2) Number of fabric widths (as figured above)	×
3) Total fabric length	=
4) Number of yds. (meters) needed: total fabric length divided by 36" (100 cm)	yds. (m)

*Round up to the nearest whole number.

NOTE: Add extra fabric for straightening ends.

NOTE: Half of the width (determined above) will be used for each curtain panel. To piece panels, adjust width measurement to include 1" (2.5 cm) for each seam.

Cutting & Matching

Cut fabric on the true lengthwise and crosswise grain to *square* the ends. Squaring ensures that curtains will always hang straight. Most fabrics should be squared by pulling a thread on the crosswise grain and cutting along the thread.

Avoid prints that are obviously off-grain. If these fabrics are cut on-grain, the design motif will be crooked and impossible to match at seams and edges. Many prints and woven patterns are only slightly off-grain, but their unevenness may be more apparent once the curtains are hung. Square the ends of these fabrics by cutting on a line of the design rather than on the crosswise grain.

Most decorator fabrics have a permanent finish which holds the threads in place. Chintz, polished cotton and other permanent-finish fabrics can be squared by simply cutting straight across the ends.

To obtain the desired finished curtain width, you may need to seam several widths of fabric together. Match the design motif of the fabric carefully so that seams are as inconspicuous as possible.

Three Ways to Straighten Crosswise Ends

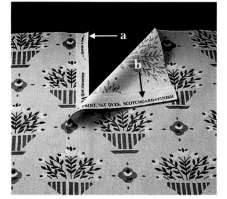

Pull one or two threads across the width of the fabric, from selvage to selvage. Cut on the line that appears after threads have been pulled out.

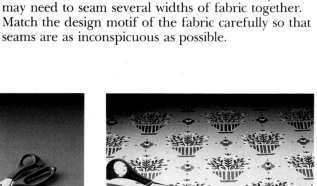

Use a carpenter's square to straighten fabrics with a permanent finish. Place one side of square parallel to selvage. Mark along other side of square; cut on marked line. Or align selvage with corner of table; cut across end.

Locate a design that runs straight across the fabric on the crosswise grain. Cut along the design. Consider depth of hem or heading when determining placement of the design on the finished curtain.

Tips for Matching Design Motifs

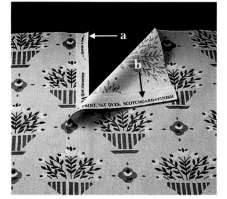

Match motifs at the selvage when using decorator fabrics. Motifs on these fabrics are split evenly at the selvage **(a)** for matching widths easily. Press under one selvage and lap it over the matching motif **(b)**. Stitch or fuse seam.

Use fusible web to align motifs for stitching. Press under one seam allowance. Place fusing strips on opposite seam allowance. Match design from right side and press lightly with dry iron. Turn fused seam to wrong side and stitch.

Match motifs from wrong side by placing point of pin through matching design details. Pin at close intervals to prevent shifting. Stitch using Even Feed™ foot to keep seam aligned, removing pins as you come to them.

Hemming

If you have measured, figured and cut accurately, your curtains should fit windows perfectly once they are hemmed. For the neatest and easiest hems, follow the procedure used in professional workrooms: sew the lower hems first, the side hems next, and casings and headings last.

Side and lower hems of unlined curtains are almost always double to provide strength, weight and stability. The easiest way to make a double-fold hem is to press it in place on an ironing board or padded work surface. Use a seam gauge to measure each fold. As you make the fold, pin the fabric to the padding, placing the pins so they do not interfere with pressing. If side edges are on the selvage, cut off selvage or clip it at 1" (2.5 cm) intervals.

Curtains hang better when hems are weighted or anchored. Sew small weights into the hems at the lower corners and bottoms of seams to keep the curtain from pulling or puckering. Use heavier weights for full-length curtains, lighter weights for lightweight fabrics and shorter curtains.

How to Sew Double-fold Hems

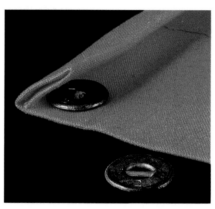

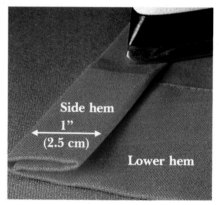

1) Turn a scant 3" (7.5 cm) to wrong side on lower edge of curtain. Pin along cut edge. Press fold. Turn under another 3" (7.5 cm), pin and press in place. Finish lower hem using one of the methods below.

2) Turn a scant 1" (2.5 cm) to the wrong side for side hems. Pin and press. Fold under another 1" (2.5 cm); pin and press. Tack weights inside the second fold at seams and side corners, if desired.

3) Press the side hems in place. When the hems have been pressed, finish them with straight stitching, machine blindstitching or fusible web.

Three Ways to Finish Curtain Hems

Straight-stitch on folded hem edge, using 8 to 10 stitches per inch (2.5 cm). When stitching three layers of fabric, lessen pressure slightly and stitch slowly.

Machine blindstitch to make stitches almost invisible on right side. After pressing, fold hem back to right side, leaving a fold of fabric ⅛" (3 mm) from hem edge. Set machine to blindstitch. Adjust zigzag stitch to take tiny bite into curtain only.

Fuse hem in place. Tuck strip of fusible web between pressed hem and curtain. Follow manufacturer's instructions for fusing, using damp press cloth for additional steam. Most fusibles require 15 seconds for permanent bonding.

Casings & Headings

A casing or *rod pocket* is the hem along the upper edge of the curtain or valance. The curtain rod is inserted through the casing so that the fullness of the curtain falls into soft gathers.

Before cutting the curtains, decide on the casing style. A simple casing places the curtain rod at the uppermost edge of the curtain.

For simple casings, add to the cut length an amount equal to the diameter of the rod plus ½" (1.3 cm) to turn under and ¼" to 1" (6 mm to 2.5 cm) ease. The amount of ease depends on the size of the rod and thickness of the fabric.

A heading is a gathered edge above the casing. It finishes the curtain more decoratively than a simple casing. Curtains with headings do not require cornices or valances.

For casings with headings, use the formula for a simple casing, adding to it an amount twice the depth of the heading. Headings may be from 1" to 5" (2.5 to 12.5 cm) deep. The depth of the heading

must be determined before the curtains are cut. The heading depth should be appropriate for the length of the curtain: in general, the longer the curtain, the deeper the heading.

Wooden, brass or plastic poles may be covered with a *shirred pole cover*. The exposed pole between the curtain panels is covered with a casing made from a shirred tube of matching fabric (above). The casing may be plain or have a heading the same height as the curtain heading. Wide poles and casings are more than decorative. They often are used to conceal a shade heading, the plain heading on shirred curtains, or the traverse rod of sheer or lightweight curtains.

Wide casings are used on the flat *Continental™ rod* or *cornice rod*. These rods are 4½" (11.5 cm) wide. A cornice rod is actually two regular curtain rods attached with a spacer between them.

Finish lower and side hems of curtains before sewing casings and headings.

How to Sew a Simple Casing

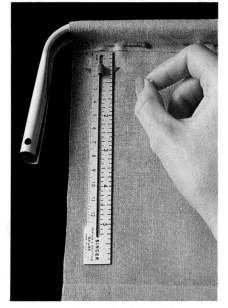

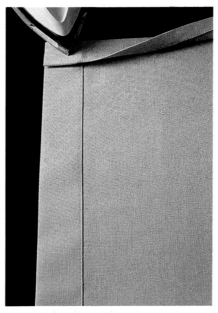

1) Determine casing depth by loosely pinning a curtain fabric strip around the rod. Remove rod and measure the distance from the top of the strip to the pin. Add ½" (1.3 cm) to be turned under.

2) Press under ½" (1.3 cm) along upper cut edge of curtain panel. Fold over again and press to form a hem equal to amount measured in step 1.

3) Stitch close to folded hem edge to form casing, backstitching at both ends. If desired, stitch again close to the upper edge to create a sharp crease appropriate for flat or oval curtain rods.

How to Sew a Casing with a Heading

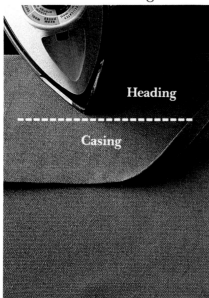

1) Determine the depth of the casing and the heading as directed in step 1, above. Press under ½" (1.3 cm) along upper cut edge of the curtain panel. Fold and press again to form hem equal to casing plus heading depth.

2) Stitch close to folded hem edge, backstitching at both ends. Mark heading depth with a pin at each end of panel. Stitch again at marked depth. To aid straight stitching, apply a strip of masking tape to the bed of the machine at heading depth, or use seam guide.

3) Insert rod through casing and gather curtain evenly onto rod. Adjust heading by pulling up the folded edge so the seam is exactly on the lower edge of the rod. A wide heading may be made to look puffy and more rounded by pulling the fabric out on each side.

How to Sew a Continental™ or Cornice Rod Casing with a Heading

1) Measure window after Continental or cornice rod has been installed to determine total length. Add 15½" (39.3 cm): 5½" (14 cm) for casing and turned hem, 8" (20.5 cm) for double-fold hem, and 2" (5 cm) for heading. If deeper heading is desired, add twice the heading depth.

2) Turn under ½" (1.3 cm) on upper edge of curtain and press. Fold over again to form a 6" (15 cm) double-fold hem. Stitch 1" (2.5 cm) from upper folded edge to form ruffle heading. Stitch close to folded hem edge to form casing.

3) Insert rod through casing and gather curtain evenly onto rod. Hang on installed brackets. For a dramatic wide heading on floor-length curtains, use two Continental or cornice rods, installed one above the other. Add 12" (30.5 cm) for second casing.

How to Make a Shirred Pole Cover

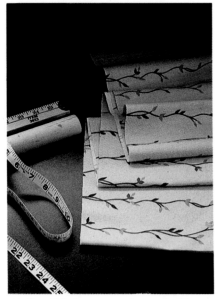

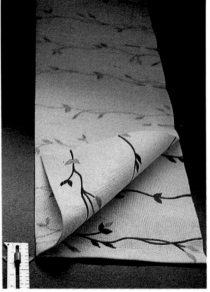

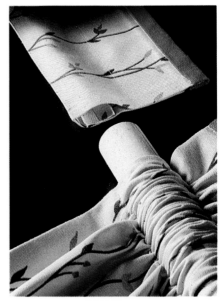

1) Cut fabric two and one-half times the length of pole area to be covered; cut width equal to circumference of pole plus 1½" (3.8 cm). For pole cover with a heading, add amount equal to twice the heading depth.

2) Stitch ½" (1.3 cm) hems on short ends. Fold strip in half lengthwise, right sides together, and pin long edges together. Stitch ½" (1.3 cm) seam. Press seam open. Turn cover right side out.

3) Press cover so that seam is at back of pole. To form heading, stitch again at appropriate distance from upper folded edge. Gather pole cover onto rod between two curtain panels.

Customizing Casing-top Curtains

Bindings, borders, ribbon or contrasting returns give casings individuality and style. These decorative touches customize casings and require little additional sewing time.

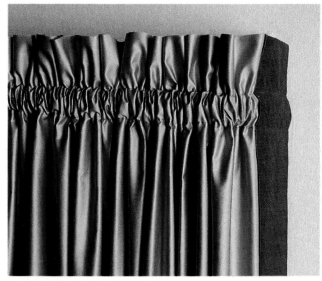

Contrasting return. Cut strips of contrasting fabric the width of rod return plus 1" (2.5 cm) for seams. Press under ½" (1.3 cm) on one long side. Pin strip to unfinished side of curtain, wrong sides together, raw edges aligned. Stitch ½" (1.3 cm) seam. Turn and press strip to right side; fuse or topstitch to right side of curtain.

Narrow binding. Cut 1½" (3.8 cm) wide strips of coordinating fabric. Press under ½" (1.3 cm) on one long side. Pin unpressed edge of strip to hemmed curtain, right sides together. Stitch ½" (1.3 cm) seam. Press folded edge of binding up and over hemmed edge. From right side, stitch in the ditch (the groove created at first seam).

Topstitched ribbon banding. Cut geometric bands or ribbon-type trims from coordinating fabric, the width of finished band plus 1" (2.5 cm). Press under ½" (1.3 cm) on both sides of banding; pin 1" to 2" (2.5 to 5 cm) from hemmed edge. Edgestitch both sides of band in same direction, close to each folded edge. Use Even Feed™ foot to aid smooth stitching.

Fused border. Cut stripes or border from coordinating striped wallpaper-type print, allowing ½" (1.3 cm) on each side for finishing. Press under ½" (1.3 cm) on both sides of border. Cut strips of fusible web, slightly narrower than finished trim. Insert web between hemmed curtains and border. Fuse in place, following manufacturer's instructions.

Lining Curtains

Linings add body and weight to curtains to help them hang better. A lining also adds opaqueness, prevents fading and sun damage to curtain fabric, and provides some insulation. Patterned and colored curtains should be lined to give windows a uniform look from the outside of the house.

Select linings according to the weight of the curtain fabric. White or off-white sateen is the most often used lining fabric. Specially treated linings which resist staining and block out light are also available.

For a lined curtain with a casing, cut the curtain as directed on page 27, including a 4" (10 cm) double-fold hem. Cut lining fabric 6" (15 cm) narrower and 5½" (14 cm) shorter than the cut curtain. Seam and press widths and part widths, aligning curtain seams with lining seams where possible.

Curtains can also be lined to the edge to create a custom look. Cut the lining the same length and width as the curtain; use coordinating fabric for contrast along the edge of the curtain.

How to Line Curtains

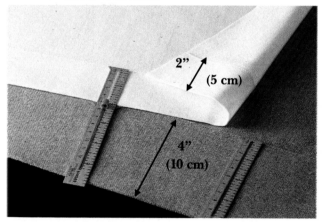

1) **Turn,** press and stitch a 2" (5 cm) double-fold hem in lining. Turn, press and stitch 4" (10 cm) double-fold hem in curtain. On wrong side of curtain, measure finished length from hem to upper edge of curtain; mark with line parallel to cut edge. Lining will end at this mark.

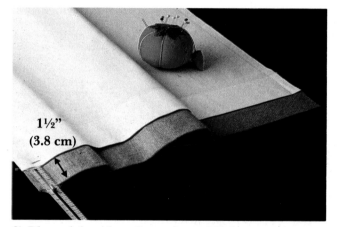

2) **Place** right sides of curtain and lining together so that lining hem is 1½" (3.8 cm) above curtain hem. Pin and stitch ½" (1.3 cm) seams on sides.

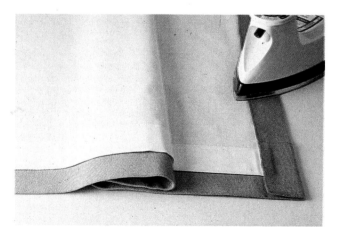

3) **Place** curtain face down on flat surface. Center lining on top of curtain so an equal amount of curtain is turned back on each side of lining. Press side seams toward lining.

4) **Turn** curtain right side out. Center lining so side hems are equal width. Align upper edge of lining with finished length marking on curtain. Carefully press side hems. At unfinished upper edges, press under amount equal to side hems.

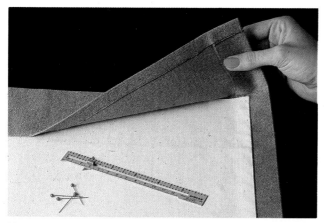

5) Turn upper edge of curtain down along lining to form casing and heading, if used. Stitch casing.

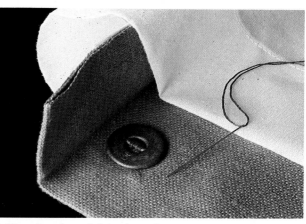

6) Hand-tack weights along lower edge of curtain inside side hems and seams.

7) Turn side hems back diagonally below lining to form a miter. Slipstitch miter in place.

8) Make French tacks, about 12" (30.5 cm) apart, between hem and lining. Use double thread. Take two stitches near top of hem and directly across in lining, leaving 1" (2.5 cm) slack in thread. Blanket stitch over thread. Secure with knot in lining.

How to Line Curtains to the Edge

1) Cut curtain and lining the same size. Turn, press and stitch equal lower hems in curtain and lining. Place right sides of curtain and lining together with lower hems even. Pin sides and upper edge.

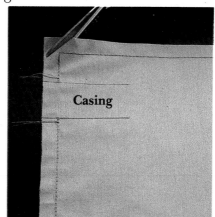

Casing

2) Mark casing and heading depth on lining. Join lining and curtain with ½" (1.3 cm) seam on sides and upper edge, leaving opening on both sides at casing line. Diagonally trim upper corners. Press the upper seam open.

3) Turn curtain right side out. Press seams flat. Stitch casing and heading. Insert curtain rod in casing. Hang curtain and fold lining to right side to create trimmed edge.

Tab Top Curtains

Fabric tabs are an attractive alternative to conventional casings or curtain rings. Tab top curtains create a traditional country look, a contemporary tailored look or a casual cafe look. They are also ideal for stationary side panels. Tabs give top interest to a curtain, and can be made with contrasting fabric, decorative ribbon or trim.

Only one and one-half to two times fullness is needed for tab top curtains. When determining the finished length, the upper edge of the curtain should be 1½" to 2" (3.8 to 5 cm) below the rod. This determines the length of the tabs. Determine number of tabs needed by placing a tab at each edge of the curtain, and one in the center. Space the remaining tabs 6" to 8" (15 to 20.5 cm) apart.

Allow ½" (1.3 cm) at the upper edge of curtain instead of the usual casing allowance. Stitch double-fold side and lower hems (page 29), then proceed as directed below.

How to Sew Tab Top Curtains

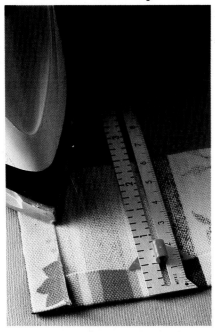

1) Cut a 3" (7.5 cm) facing strip equal in length to the width of the curtain panel. Press under ½" (1.3 cm) on one long side and each short end.

2) Measure tab length by pinning a strip of fabric over the rod and marking the desired length with a pin. Add ½" (1.3 cm) for seam allowance. Cut tabs the desired length, and two times the desired width plus 1" (2.5 cm).

3) Fold each tab in half lengthwise, right sides together. Stitch ½" (1.3 cm) seam along cut edge, using continuous stitching (arrow) to sew from one tab to the next. Turn tabs right side out. Center seam in back of each tab and press.

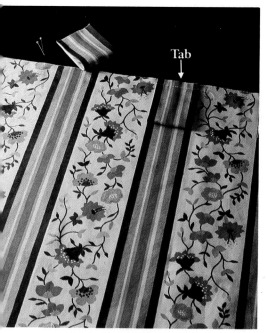

4) Fold each tab in half so that raw edges are aligned. Pin or baste tabs in place on right side of curtain, aligning raw edges of tabs with upper edge of curtain. Place end tabs even with finished side edges of curtain.

5) Pin facing strip to upper edge of curtain, right sides together, so that raw edges are aligned and tabs are sandwiched between facing and curtain. Stitch ½" (1.3 cm) seam.

6) Press facing to wrong side of curtain so that tabs extend upward. Slipstitch or fuse side and lower edges of facing to curtain. Insert decorative curtain rod through tabs.

Ruffled Curtains

Ruffled curtains add a charming, warm touch to any room of the house. Ruffles are functional as well as decorative; their weight helps curtains hang better.

Ruffle fullness depends on fabric weight and ruffle width. Sheer fabrics usually need triple fullness; crisper fabrics need only two or two and one-half times fullness. Wide ruffles should be fuller than narrow ruffles. You will usually need to purchase less additional fabric when ruffles are cut on the crosswise grain. If ruffles are cut on the selvage, use the selvage edge in the seam. Hem edge of ruffle before gathering.

Single ruffles are one layer of gathered fabric with a hemmed edge. Narrow ruffles should have a hem no wider than ¼" (6 mm).

Double ruffles require a double width of fabric which is folded in half, wrong sides together. The folded edge eliminates the need for a hem. Because of the extra bulk created by two layers, it is best to make double ruffles from lightweight fabrics.

Making ruffles can be time consuming, so use time and energy savers whenever possible. The zigzag stitch, the ruffler and the narrow hemmer can speed up the task. Begin by cutting the fabric the appropriate width for a single or double ruffle. Then seam sections together at the short ends to make a continuous length, using plain seams for double ruffles and French seams for single ruffles. Hem one long edge of single ruffles, either by machine-stitching a double-fold ¼" (6 mm) hem, or by using a narrow hemmer.

Two Timesaving Ways to Make Ruffles

Zigzag over a strong, thin cord to make long ruffles easier to adjust into even gathers. Use string, crochet cotton or dental floss, placed ⅜" (1 cm) from raw edge. Use wide zigzag setting so cord does not get caught in the stitching.

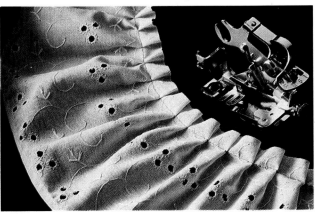

Use a ruffler attachment to gather as you sew. Make a test strip and adjust ruffler to desired fullness. Measure the test strip before and after stitching to determine length of fabric needed. Omit steps 1 through 3 (opposite) when using ruffler.

How to Attach Ruffles

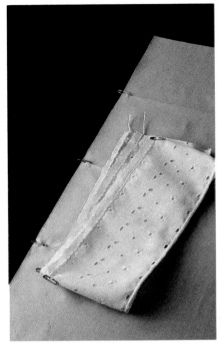

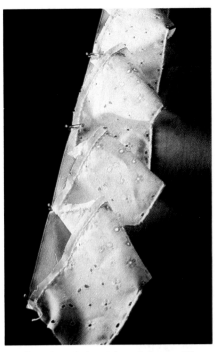

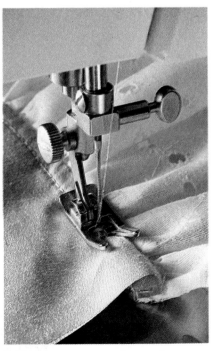

1) Divide the ruffle strip (before gathering) into fourths and mark fold lines with pins. Divide the curtain edge into fourths and mark with pins. Do not hem the edge of the curtain where the ruffles will be attached.

2) Pin the right side of the ruffle strip to the right side of the curtain, matching marking pins on the ruffle strip to marking pins on the curtain edge.

3) Pull up the gathering cord until the ruffle is the same size as the ungathered edge of the curtain.

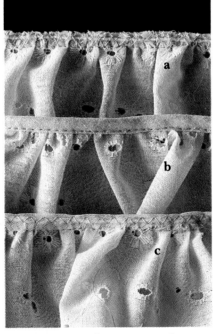

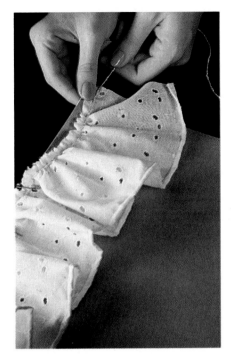

4) Pin in place as necessary to distribute gathers evenly. Stitch a ½" (1.3 cm) seam, gathered side up, controlling gathers with fingers on each side of the needle.

5) Trim seam allowances and zigzag overedge **(a)**, or encase seam with double-fold bias tape **(b)**, or encase seam with lightweight bias tricot strips **(c)**.

6) Press seam toward curtain. Topstitch on curtain side ¼" (6 mm) from seam. This helps ruffles lie smooth and even.

Tiebacks

Tiebacks are a decorative, practical way to hold curtains open. Make them straight or shaped, ruffled or plain in matching or contrasting solids, coordinating prints or bordered fabrics. Interface all tiebacks to add stability.

To make straight tiebacks the proper length, complete and hang the curtains before sewing the tiebacks. Cut a strip of fabric 2" to 4" (5 to 10 cm) wide and experiment with pinning it around the curtains to determine the best tieback length. Slide the strip up and down to find the best location, and mark the wall to position the cup hooks that fasten the tiebacks. Remove the strip and measure it to determine the finished size.

✂ Cutting Directions

For straight tiebacks, cut fabric the finished length and width plus ½" (1.3 cm) on all sides for seams.

For shaped tiebacks, cut a strip of brown paper for pattern, 4" to 6" (10 to 15 cm) wide and slightly longer than the tieback. Pin the paper around the curtain and draw a curved shape around the edge of the paper. Experiment with pinning and trimming the paper to get the effect you want. Add ½" (1.3 cm) for seams when cutting tiebacks from the pattern.

Cut strips of heavyweight fusible interfacing the same size as the *finished* tieback.

YOU WILL NEED

Decorator fabric for tiebacks.

Heavyweight fusible interfacing.

Brown paper for pattern.

Fusible web strips, length of finished tieback width.

Two ⅝" (1.5 cm) brass or plastic rings for each tieback.

Two cup hooks.

How to Sew Straight Tiebacks

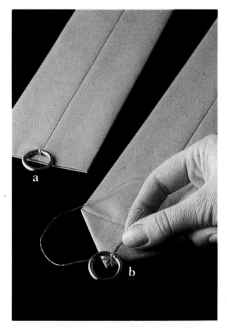

1) Center fusible interfacing on wrong side of tieback and fuse. Press ends under ½" (1.3 cm). Fold strip in half lengthwise, right sides together. Stitch ½" (1.3 cm) seam, leaving ends open. Press open.

2) Turn tieback right side out. Center seam down back and press. Turn pressed ends inside. Insert fusible web at each end and fuse or slipstitch closed.

3) Hand-tack or zigzag ring on back seamline at each end of tieback, ¼" (6 mm) from edge **(a)**. Or press corners diagonally to inside to form a point **(b)**, and slipsitich or fuse corners in place.

How to Sew Shaped Tiebacks

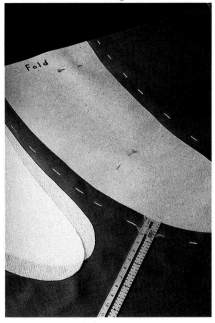

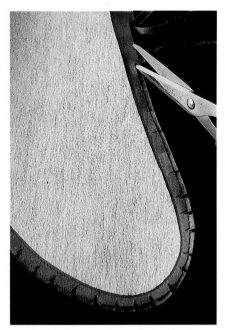

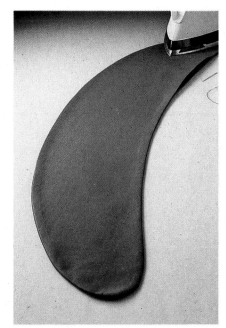

1) Cut two pieces of fusible interfacing from pattern for each tieback. Cut two pieces of fabric for each tieback, adding ½" (1.3 cm) on all sides for seam. Center interfacing on wrong side of each tieback piece and fuse.

2) Pin right sides of tieback together. Stitch ½" (1.3 cm) seam, leaving 4" (10 cm) opening on one long edge for turning. Grade seam allowances and clip or notch curves at regular intervals.

3) Turn tieback right side out; press. Slipstitch or fuse opening closed. Hand-tack or zigzag rings to ends of tieback.

Bound Tiebacks

Binding emphasizes the graceful line of a curved tieback and allows you to pick up an accent color from the room decor or from the curtain fabric. Shaped tiebacks are easier to bind than straight tiebacks because the bias will ease around curves. For straight bound tiebacks, miter corners by following directions for banded placemats (page 106). You can also add cording to a tieback by following the directions for a corded pillow (pages 74 to 75).

✂ Cutting Directions

Follow the cutting directions in step 1, below. Use purchased bias tape or make your own. Cut the tape slightly longer than the distance around the tieback.

How to Bind Shaped Tiebacks

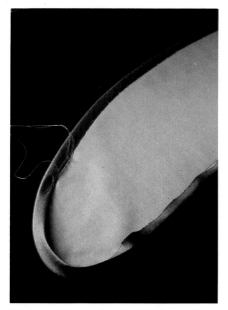

1) Cut two pieces of fabric and two pieces of fusible interfacing from pattern. Do not add a ½" (1.3 cm) seam allowance to tieback. Fuse interfacing to wrong side of tieback.

2) Pin wrong sides of tieback together. Bastestitch ⅜" (1 cm) from edge on all sides. Hand-baste right side of bias strip to right side of tieback, clipping bias to ease around curves. Stitch bias strip to tieback, ½" (1.3 cm) from edge.

3) Press bias strip over edge of tieback. Turn under cut edge of strip to meet stitching line. Slipstitch binding to seamline. Hand-tack or zigzag rings to ends of tieback.

Ruffled Tiebacks

Adding ruffles to tiebacks is another simple way to change the appearance of the curtains and the look of a window. Make ruffles from a matching or coordinating fabric in a width that suits the length of the curtain. Use purchased pregathered lace or eyelet ruffles to cut sewing time.

✂ Cutting Directions

Cut ruffle the desired width plus 1" (2.5 cm) for seams, and two and one-half times the finished length. Cut a straight tieback (page 40) in proportion to the ruffle width, usually less than half as wide.

Cut strips of heavyweight fusible interfacing the same size as the *finished* tieback.

How to Sew Ruffled Tiebacks

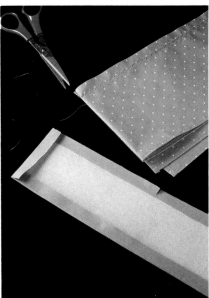

1) Fuse interfacing to wrong side of tieback. Press under ½" (1.3 cm) on one side and both ends of tieback. Stitch a ¼" (6 mm) hem on one side and both ends of ruffle. Fold ruffle and tieback into fourths; mark folds with snips.

2) Prepare ruffle for gathering (page 38). Pin wrong side of ruffle to right side of tieback, matching snips. Pull up gathering cord until ruffle fits tieback. Distribute gathers evenly and pin. Stitch ruffle ½" (1.3 cm) from edge.

3) Fold tieback in half lengthwise, wrong sides together. Pin the folded edge over ruffle seam on right side of tieback. Edgestitch across ends and along gathered seam. Hand-tack or zigzag the rings to ends of tieback.

Shower Curtain

A shower curtain is one of the simplest curtains to sew. Valances, ruffled headings and tiebacks can all be used with the standard shower curtain. Because of its size, the shower curtain is a good place to use bold colors and prints. The instructions for sewing a shower curtain can also be used for cafe curtains or straight curtains hung with curtain hooks or rings on decorative poles. (Omit eyelets, grommets and plastic shower curtain liner.)

✂ Cutting Directions

Measure the distance from the bottom of the shower rod to the desired length. Add 10" (25.5 cm) for upper and lower hems. Measure the width of the area to be covered by the curtain and add 4" (10 cm) for side hems. Standard shower curtain liners are 72" × 72" (183 × 183 cm), so the curtain should be cut 76" (193 cm) wide if using a standard liner. Seam fabric together as needed, using French seams.

YOU WILL NEED

Decorator fabric for shower curtain.

Plastic shower curtain liner.

Eyelets or grommets (not necessary if buttonholes are used), equal to number of holes in plastic liner.

Shower curtain hooks, equal to number of eyelets or buttonholes.

The fabric curtain and plastic liner can hang together on the same hooks, or separately on a shower rod and a spring tension rod. When they hang together, the shower curtain and the liner should be the same width.

How to Sew a Shower Curtain

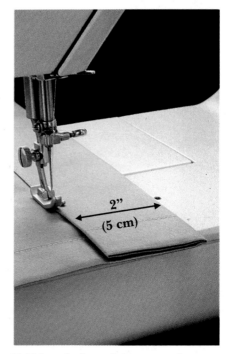

1) Turn under and stitch a 3" (7.5 cm) double-fold hem on lower edge of curtain. Turn under and stitch 1" (2.5 cm) double-fold hem on each side of the curtain.

2) Press under 2" (5 cm) double-fold hem at upper edge of curtain. Fuse 2" (5 cm) strip of fusible interfacing in second fold, 2" (5 cm) from raw edge. Interfacing adds stability and body to the finished curtain.

3) Edgestitch or fuse upper hem in place. Fusing adds more stability to upper edge of curtain. Follow manufacturer's directions when using fusible web.

4) Mark positions for eyelets, grommets or buttonholes across upper hem, using the plastic liner as the guide for spacing holes. Position liner ¼" (6 mm) down from upper edge of curtain.

5) Fasten eyelets securely using eyelet plier, or eyelet set and hammer. If using eyelet set, work on a piece of scrap wood or a hard surface that will not be damaged when pounding eyelets.

6) Make vertical buttonholes, ¼" to ½" (6 mm to 1.3 cm) long. Cut open and insert hooks. Prevent buttonholes from raveling by applying liquid fray preventer to the cut edges.

Shades

Shades control light and provide privacy when used alone or with curtains. Because they fit close to windows, shades are also energy efficient.

The Roman shade is the basis for stitched-tuck, hobbled, cloud, balloon and insulated shades. These shades are raised and lowered by a system of cords and rings which cause them to pleat into soft folds when raised.

A stitched-tuck shade has small, topstitched tucks along the folds of the shade. These tucked rows alternate between the front and the back of the shade, giving the pleats a crisp look.

The hobbled shade is twice the length of a flat Roman shade. Excess fabric is taken up in permanent soft folds between each row of rings, giving the shade a bubbled look when lowered.

The cloud shade is cut two to three times wider than the window, then shirred across the upper edge to create a soft heading. The lower edge of the shade falls into gentle poufs.

The balloon shade is also cut twice as wide as the window, but its fullness is folded into oversized inverted pleats at the heading and lower edge. This shade also has permanent poufs at the bottom.

An insulated shade is a basic Roman shade made with insulated, four-layer lining and a magnetic edge-seal. These shades block out heat or cold, and help regulate temperature extremes at windows.

A roller shade takes on a custom look when made to coordinate with fabrics in the room. These shades, stiffened with an iron-on shade backing, are easy to make because they require very little sewing.

Two Ways to Mount Shades

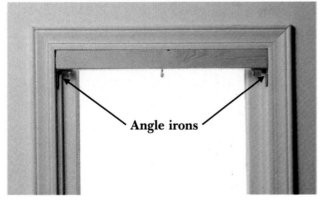

Inside mounted shade fits completely inside window opening. Accurate construction and mounting is important. Attach shade to 1"×2" (2.5 × 5 cm) mounting board, then attach board to top of window frame with angle irons or screws. Finished width and length of shade are equal to width and length of window opening.

Outside mounted shade is attached to mounting board, which is secured with screws or angle irons above the window. Finished shade is the same width as the mounting board so it covers the frame when lowered. Finished shade length equals distance from top of board to sill. Use this method for different sized or out of square windows.

Roman Shade

Roman shades have a tailored appearance that complements many styles of decor. Use them alone or add cornices, curtains or draperies.

Like roller shades, Roman shades are flat and smooth when down. When pulled up, they take up more space at the top because they pleat crisply instead of rolling. If you want the raised shade to clear the window completely, mount it at the ceiling. This also adds apparent height to the window. A system of evenly-spaced cords and rings on the back of the shade causes the shade to pleat when pulled. A weight bar near the bottom of the shade adds stability and aids smooth tracking.

The choice of fabric affects the look of the finished shade. Sturdy, firm fabrics work best for the pleats of these shades. Lightweight, softer fabrics may be used, but the shades will be less crisp-looking. Roman shades are usually lined. This gives added body to the shade, prevents fabric fading and gives the outside of the house a uniform appearance.

You may need to seam fabric or lining to create enough width for the shades. Be sure to consider these seams when measuring for construction. Additional fabric may be needed to match a print, plaid or other design.

To make measuring and construction easier and more accurate, use a folding cardboard cutting board on your work surface.

✂ Cutting Directions

Determine width and length of finished shade. Cut decorator fabric for shade 3" (7.5 cm) larger than finished shade.

Cut lining with width equal to finished width of shade; length equal to finished length plus 3" (7.5 cm).

Cut facing strip from lining fabric, 5" (12.5 cm) wide; length equal to finished width of shade plus 2" (5 cm).

YOU WILL NEED

Decorator fabric for shade.

Lining fabric for lining and facing strip.

Mounting board, 1" × 2" (2.5 × 5 cm), long enough for inside or outside mounting (page 47).

Plastic rings, ½" (1.3 cm) or ⅝" (1.5 cm), equal to number of vertical rows multiplied by number of horizontal rows. Or use purchased ring tape with 6" (15 cm) spaces.

Screw eyes or pulleys, large enough to accommodate all the pull cords. Number should equal the number of vertical rows.

Nylon cable cord for each vertical row of rings. Each cord must be long enough to go up the shade, across the top and partway down the side for pulling.

Weight rod, one ⅜" (1 cm) brass rod or ½" (1.3 cm) rustproof flat bar, cut ½" (1.3 cm) shorter than finished width of shade.

White glue or liquid fray preventer.

Awning cleat.

Staple gun or tacks.

Drapery pull (optional).

How to Make a Roman Shade

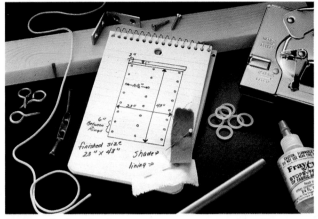

1) Sketch the shade to use as pattern guide. Show hems and ring locations. Cut shade; seam for width, if necessary. If fabric ravels, finish side edges with zigzag stitch or liquid fray preventer.

2) Place shade fabric wrong side up on work surface. Mark finished width. Turn in equal side hems, about 1½" (3.8 cm), and press.

3) Place lining on shade fabric, wrong sides together. Mark and cut to fit unfinished length and finished width of shade. Slip lining under side hems. Smooth and press lining. Pin in place.

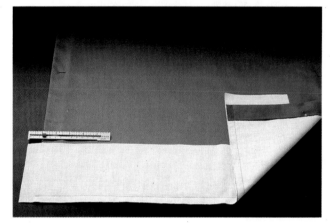

4) Center and pin facing strip on right side of shade, even with lower edge, with 1" (2.5 cm) extending at each side. Stitch ½" (1.3 cm) from lower edge. Press toward wrong side of shade.

5) Fold and press facing extensions to back of shade so they do not show on the right side. Fuse, tack or slipstitch in place.

6) Turn under raw edge of facing 1½" (3.8 cm). Then turn under to make a 3" (7.5 cm) hem. Stitch along folded edge. Stitch again, 1" (2.5 cm) from first stitching to form weight rod pocket.

(Continued on next page.)

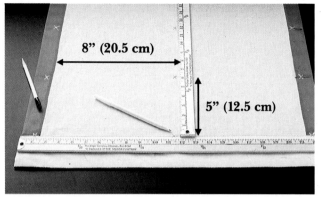

7) Mark positions for rings with horizontal and vertical rows of X's. First, mark outside vertical rows 1" (2.5 cm) from shade edges so rings hold side hems in place. Space vertical rows 8" to 12" (20.5 to 30.5 cm) apart across shade. Then, position bottom row just above the weight rod pocket. Space horizontal rows 5" to 8" (12.5 to 20.5 cm) apart.

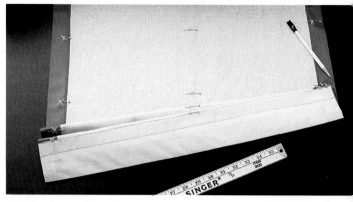

8) Pin through both layers of fabric at center of ring markings, with pins parallel to bottom of shade. Fold shade in accordion pleats at pins to position shade for machine or hand stitching of rings. If using ring tape, omit steps 9 and 10.

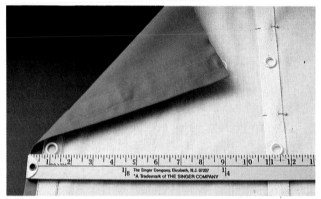

11) Ring tape can be used instead of rings. Preshrink it first. Pin tape to shade in vertical rows, making sure rings line up horizontally. Stitch along both long edges and bottom of tape with zipper foot, stitching all tapes in the same direction.

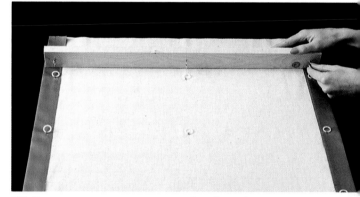

12) Insert screw eyes on mounting board to correspond with vertical rows. Place one screw eye above each row of rings. On very heavy or very wide shades, use small pulleys instead of screw eyes.

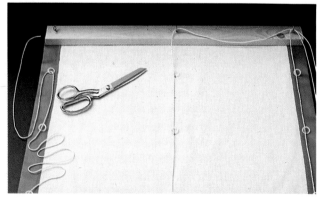

15) Cut lengths of cord, one for each row of rings. Each cord will be a different length; cords go up the shade, across the top and partway down one side. String cord through rings and screw eyes, with excess cord at one side for pulling.

16) Insert weight rod into rod pocket and slipstitch or fuse ends closed. File ends of rod or cover ends with tape before inserting. A galvanized or iron rod, painted to resist rusting, can be used instead of a brass rod.

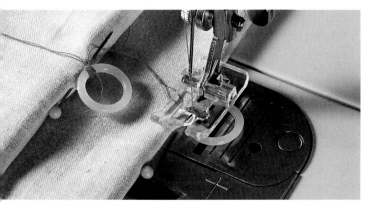

9) Attach rings by placing fold (pin in center) under presser foot with ring next to fold. Set stitch length at 0, and zigzag at widest setting. Secure ring with 8 to 10 stitches, catching small amount of fold in each stitch. Lock stitches by adjusting needle to penetrate fabric in one place (width setting at 0) for 2 or 3 stitches.

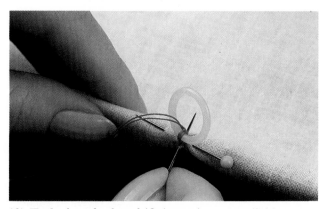

10) Tack rings by hand if zigzag is not available. Use double thread. Secure with 4 or 5 stitches in one place, through both fabric layers. Reinforce all bottom rings with extra stitches; they hold the weight of the fabric.

13) Staple or tack shade to top of mounting board. If shade is mounted outside of window frame, paint or wrap the board with lining fabric before attaching shade. This gives the shade a finished look.

14) Tie a non-slip knot in bottom ring before threading cord through the vertical row of rings. Add a dab of white glue to knot and ends of cord to prevent knot from slipping out.

17) Mount shade. Adjust cords with shade lowered so the tension on each cord is equal. Tie cords in a knot just below screw eye. Braid cords and secure at bottom with a knot or drapery pull.

18) Center awning cleat on edge of window frame or on wall. Wind cord around cleat to secure shade position when the shade is raised.

Stitched-tuck Shade

Narrow stitched tucks along each fold line add interest to this tailored version of the Roman shade. Each tuck is ¼" (6 mm) deep, so allow an extra ½" (1.3 cm) of fabric for each fold in the finished length of shade. Read about Roman shades on pages 48 to 51 before beginning this project.

To determine the number of tucks, subtract 3" (7.5 cm) for the hem from finished length of shade. Divide this number by 3" (7.5 cm), the average spacing between tucks, to get the number of tucks. Round this figure to the nearest whole number. To determine the spacing between tucks, divide the *number of tucks* (as determined above) into the finished length of shade.

✂ Cutting Directions

Cut decorator fabric and lining as for Roman shade, adding ½" (1.3 cm) for each tuck to the length of both fabrics. Also cut facing strip from lining fabric, 5" (12.5 cm) wide; length equal to finished width plus 2" (5 cm).

YOU WILL NEED

Decorator fabric for shade.

Lining fabric for lining and facing strip.

Notions: mounting board, plastic rings, screws eyes or pulleys, nylon cable cord, weight rod, white glue, awning cleat and staple gun as for Roman shade.

How to Make a Stitched-tuck Shade

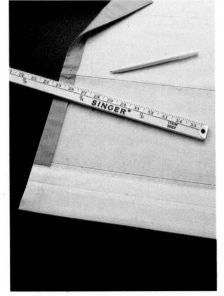

1) Follow directions for Roman shade (pages 49 and 50, steps 1 to 7). Draw lines horizontally across wrong side of shade at each line marking ring locations. Machine-baste lining and outer fabric together on marked line.

2) Fold and press sharp crease exactly on each baste-marked line, wrong side out, to make stitching lines for front of shade. Bring opposite folds together, accordian pleat style, and press crease in each fold.

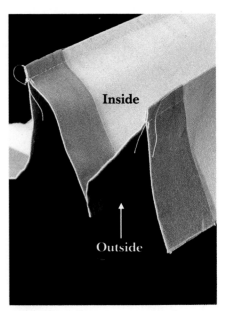

Inside

Outside

3) Machine-baste on pressed creases. Stitch tucks ¼" (6 mm) from creased edges on inside and outside of shade. Complete shade following directions for Roman shade (pages 50 and 51, steps 9 to 18). Do not use ring tape.

Hobbled Shade

The hobbled shade falls into soft folds because it is twice the length of the Roman shade. The folds are held in place by twill tape. Read about Roman shades (pages 48 to 51) before beginning this project.

To determine the number of folds, subtract 3" (7.5 cm) for the hem from finished length of shade. Divide this number by 6" (15 cm), the average spacing between folds, to get the number of folds. Round this figure to the nearest whole number. To determine the spacing between folds, divide the *number of folds* (as determined above) into the finished length of the shade.

✂ Cutting Directions

Cut decorator fabric and lining as for Roman shade, doubling the length for both fabrics. Cut facing strip from lining fabric, 5" (12.5 cm) wide; length equal to finished shade width plus 2" (5 cm). Cut twill tape, length equal to finished shade length plus 3" (7.5 cm).

YOU WILL NEED

Decorator fabric for shade.

Lining fabric for lining and facing strip.

Twill tape ½" (1.3 cm) wide.

Notions: mounting board, plastic rings, screw eyes or pulleys, nylon cable cord, weight rod, white glue, awning cleat and staple gun as for Roman shade.

How to Make a Hobbled Shade

1) Follow directions for Roman shade (pages 49 and 50, steps 1 to 7). Align tapes with shade; mark tapes every 3" (7.5 cm) or half the distance between rings on shade, beginning 1" (2.5 cm) above the rod pocket.

2) Pin tapes to the shade, matching marks on the tapes to the corresponding marks on the shade. The excess fabric between the markings forms folds on the outside of the shade.

3) Tack the rings in place, catching the tape and both layers of the fabric at each ring. Complete shade following directions for Roman shade (pages 50 and 51, steps 12 to 18).

Cloud Shade

The cloud shade is another easy-to-make variation of the Roman shade with a soft shirred heading. Because this shade has a light, airy look, lining is usually not necessary. Lightweight, soft or sheer fabrics are suggested for cloud shades.

Cloud shades are generally mounted inside the window and may be used alone or with curtains. The shade's shirred heading has a finished look that makes a valance or cornice unnecessary. A short cloud shade may also be used as a valance over other window treatments.

Cloud shades made of lightweight fabrics may be shirred on a wooden pole or curtain rod, omitting the need for a mounting board. In this case, finish the upper edge of the shade with a simple casing (page 31).

Directions for making a cloud shade are given on pages 56 and 57. Before beginning this project, read about a Roman shade on pages 48 to 51.

✂ Cutting Directions

Cut decorator fabric and seam, if necessary, so width of shade is two to two and one-half times width of window and about 12" (30.5 cm) longer than window. Also cut mounting flap 4" (10 cm) wide; the length equal to the width of the finished shade.

YOU WILL NEED

Decorator fabric for shade and mounting flap.

Four-cord shirring tape, length equal to width of shade.

Notions: mounting board, plastic rings, screw eyes or pulleys, nylon cable cord, weight rod, white glue, awning cleat and staple gun as for Roman shade.

Balloon Shade

The balloon shade is another variation of the Roman shade. A series of evenly placed box pleats gives this shade a fuller, softer effect than the more tailored Roman shade.

Made from soft, sheer or unlined fabrics, balloon shades drape into gentle poufs or swags. With sturdier fabrics, the shade's softness remains but the fabric may require hand dressing to even out the shade's fullness.

Linings are optional. Follow directions for a lined Roman shade (page 49) if opaqueness or additional body is required.

Directions for making a balloon shade are given on pages 56 and 57. Before beginning this project, read about a Roman shade on pages 48 to 51.

✂ Cutting Directions

Cut decorator fabric and seam, if necessary, so width of shade is two to two and one-half times width of window and about 12" (30.5 cm) longer than window. Also cut facing strip 1" (2.5 cm) longer than width of finished shade and 3" (7.5 cm) wide.

Make a paper pattern to help you position the pleats accurately on the shade. Make pattern by cutting a narrow strip of paper the same length as the unfinished width of the shade. (Adding machine paper works well.)

YOU WILL NEED

Decorator fabric for shade and facing strip.

Lining fabric for lining (optional).

Notions: mounting board, plastic rings, screw eyes or pulleys, nylon cable cord, weight rod, white glue, awning cleat and staple gun as for Roman shade.

How to Make a Cloud Shade

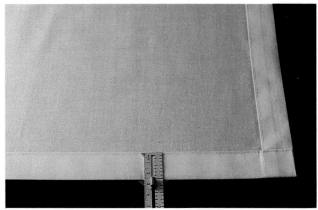

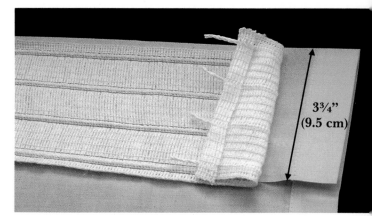

1) Seam fabric if necessary for width, using French seams. For side hems, turn under and press ½" (1.3 cm) then 1" (2.5 cm). For lower hem, turn under and press ½" (1.3 cm) then 1" (2.5 cm). Straight-stitch or blindstitch hems.

2) Turn under 3¾" (9.5 cm) at upper edge of shade. Pin 4-cord shirring tape ¼" (6 mm) from folded edge. Pull out ½" (1.3 cm) of cording at each end; turn tape under to finish ends. Using zipper foot, stitch across shade above and below each cord.

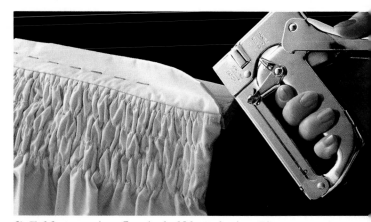

5) Pull other ends of cords until shade gathers up to width of mounting board. Knot, glue and trim pulled cord ends as in step 4, above.

6) Fold mounting flap in half lengthwise. Pin raw edges of flap to right side of shade above shirring tape and stitch ½" (1.3 cm) from edge. Staple folded edge of flap to top of mounting board.

How to Make a Balloon Shade

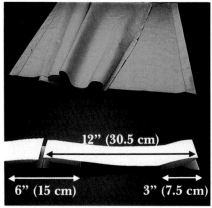

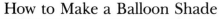

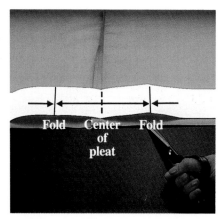

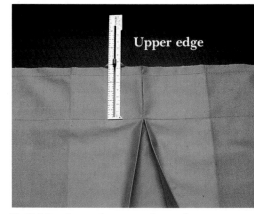

1) Prepare fabric as above, step 1, but do not hem lower edge. Fold pleats in pattern 9" to 12" (23 to 30.5 cm) apart and about 6" (15 cm) deep. Use even number of pleats with half pleat at each side.

2) Place paper pattern on shade at lower edge. Place seams at back folds of pleats. Mark pleat fold lines with ¼" (6 mm) snips. Repeat this step along the upper edge of the shade.

3) Fold, pin and press pleats the entire length of shade. Stitch across shade ½" (1.3 cm) from upper and lower edges to secure pleats. Stitch again 3" (7.5 cm) from upper edge for mounting.

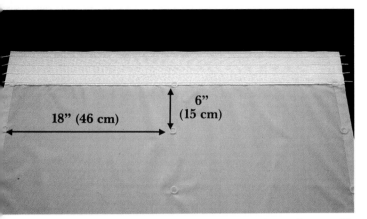

18" (46 cm)   6" (15 cm)

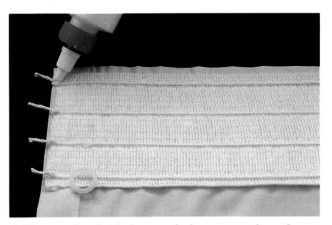

3) Mark positions for rings. Space horizontal rows 6" to 10" (15 to 25.5 cm) apart. Space vertical rows 18" to 36" (46 to 91.5 cm) apart; rows will be half that distance apart when shirring tape is gathered. Stitch or tack rings in place.

4) Knot ends of shirring cord along one edge of shade to keep the cords from pulling out. Put a small amount of white glue on knots so they stay in position. Trim ends.

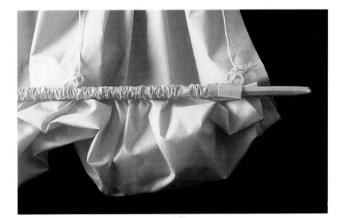

7) Tie three rings together at bottom of each vertical row. This creates a permanent pouf in the shade, even when it is completely lowered. String and mount as for Roman shades, pages 50 and 51, steps 15, 17 and 18.

8) Tape ends of weight rod to cover rough edges. Insert rod in lower hem. Gather fabric evenly on the weight rod to correspond with gathers on upper edge. On sheer fabrics, cover the weight rod with matching fabric. Slipstitch or fuse ends of hem closed.

4) Press under ½" (1.3 cm) on short ends of hem facing strip. Press strip in half lengthwise, wrong sides together. Pin strip to lower edge of shade on right side. Stitch ½" (1.3 cm) from edge.

5) Press strip to wrong side to form rod pocket and hem. Position rings at center of pleats, with bottom rings on facing fold. Space horizontal rows of rings 6" to 10" (15 to 25.5 cm) apart.

6) Staple upper edge of shade to mounting board. Finish as for cloud shade above, steps 7 and 8.

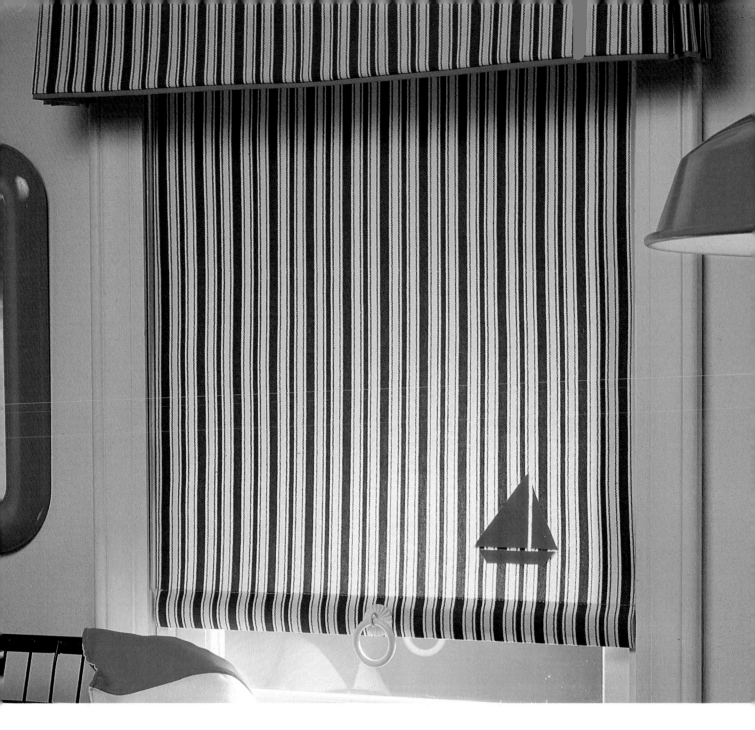

Roller Shade

Roller shades are versatile and attractive window treatments. Mount the shade inside the window opening with ¼" (6 mm) or less clearance around the edges to increase the energy efficiency of a window. Roller shades can also be hung on brackets on the frame or wall outside the window. Use a wood or steel ruler for accuracy when measuring. For inside mounting, measure from just outside one bracket projection to just outside the other. If you do not want the roller to show, reverse the brackets or use reverse brackets, and cut the roller to fit.

✂ Cutting Directions

Cut decorator fabric 1" to 2" (2.5 to 5 cm) wider than jamb or bracket measurement, and 12" (30.5 cm) longer than area to be covered top to bottom. Cut iron-on backing with same dimensions.

YOU WILL NEED

Decorator fabric and iron-on shade backing for shade.

Wood slat, ¼" (6 mm) shorter than finished width of shade.

Roller to fit window width.

Staple gun with ¼" (6 mm) staples, masking tape or other strong tape and white glue.

Shade pull (optional).

How to Make a Roller Shade

1) Mark center at upper and lower edges of decorator fabric and iron-on backing. Place wrong side of fabric to adhesive side of backing, matching edges and center markings.

2) Bond according to manufacturer's directions for time and temperature, pressing from center to outside, and from top to bottom. Let shade cool so bond is permanently set.

3) Use a yardstick to mark cutting lines on sides of shade; distance between cutting lines should be equal to finished width of shade. Use a carpenter's square or cutting board to assure right angles.

4) Cut carefully along cutting lines with smooth, even strokes. To keep edges from raveling, put a small amount of white glue on your finger and draw it along each edge. Let dry completely.

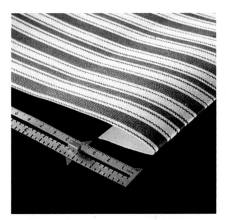

5) Fold under 1½" (3.8 cm) along lower edge for a straight hem and slat pocket. Use carpenter's square to double check right angles at corners.

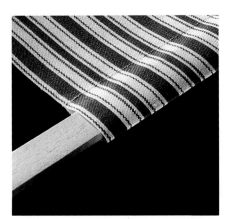

6) Stitch 1¼" (3.2 cm) from folded edge using longest stitch length to form a pocket for the slat. Press pocket. Insert the slat. Attach shade pull if desired.

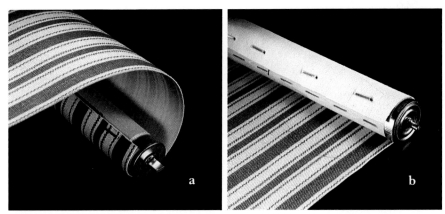

7) Position roller under or over top of shade, depending on how shade is to roll. To attach roller under shade, place flat pin to the right **(a)**; to attach roller over shade, place round pin to the right **(b)**. Make sure wrong side of hem is turned so it will not show when shade is hung. Staple or tape shade to roller.

Insulated Roman Shade

Insulated Roman shades make good sense for energy-conscious sewers. These practical shades help your home stay warm in the winter and cool in the summer and pay for themselves in reduced heating and cooling costs. Read about Roman shades on pages 48 to 51 before beginning this project.

The shades are lined with insulated lining, the portion of the shade which provides effective insulation when the shade is lowered. The lining can also be used for other energy-saving projects like special draperies and window mats. Insulated lining consists of four layers (see below), quilted in 8" (20.5 cm) channels, with 4" (10 cm) channels at the edges.

Because the insulating layers are quilted, the time-consuming task of making your own layers is eliminated. Quilting also reduces bulk, making the finished shade more attractive and easier to handle.

The quilting lines mark the horizontal ring positions on the Roman shade. (Channels run on *lengthwise* grain but *crosswise* on the finished shade.) This eliminates much of the measuring normally required to mark ring positions.

Combined with an edge-seal system, insulated shades can reduce heat loss and heat gain from windows even more effectively. An edge-seal system consists of flexible magnetic strips placed along the sides of the window and inside the shade edges. On closed shades, these strips form an airtight seal which keeps warm, moist air from flowing around the edges of the shade, causing energy loss and condensation.

Before making the shade, decide how it will be mounted to determine the length and width of the finished shade. The three types of mounts that may be used for insulated Roman shades are *inside, outside* and *hybrid*. Descriptions of inside and outside mounts are given on pages 47 and 64.

The hybrid mount (page 64) is especially good for insulated shades. Although the mounting board is cut and mounted like an inside mount, the shade is wider and overlaps the window to control airflow around the edges.

✂ Cutting Directions

Cut fabric for shade 3" (7.5 cm) wider and 12" (30.5 cm) longer than finished shade. Cut lining with width equal to finished width of shade; length equal to finished length plus 4" (10 cm) for mounting ease.

YOU WILL NEED

Decorator fabric for shade.

Insulated lining, channel quilted.

Magnetic tape for edge-seal system.

Notions: Mounting board, plastic rings, screw eyes, pulley or pulley lock, nylon cable cord, weight rod, awning cleat, glue and staple gun, as for Roman shade.

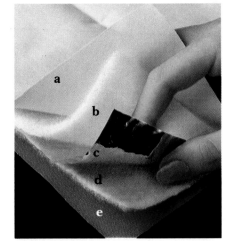

Insulated lining consists of four layers: cotton/polyester lining, right side (**a**); polyester batting (**b**); polyethelene moisture vapor barrier (**c**); heat-reflecting Mylar®(**d**). With the addition of the decorator fabric (**e**), the shade provides five layers of insulation.

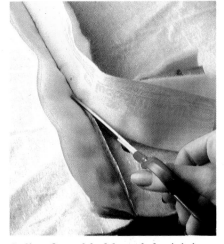

Splice for added length by joining two pieces on quilting lines. This maintains 8" (20.5 cm) between lines. Stitch through all layers, applying slight tension in front of and behind needle. Trim and grade seam to ¼" (6 mm), holding scissors at an angle.

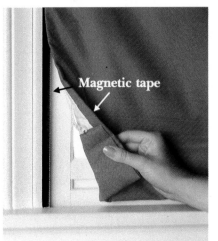

Edge-seal system consists of strips of magnetic tape placed on the window frame to correspond to strips of tape placed inside the shade. When pressed together, magnets form a seal that shuts out hot or cold air. To release seal, pull shade out at lower edge.

How to Sew an Insulated Roman Shade

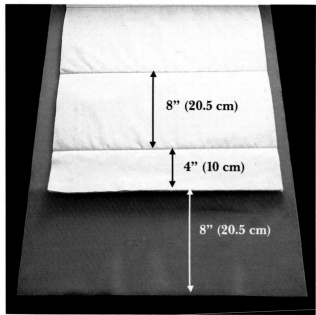

8" (20.5 cm)

4" (10 cm)

8" (20.5 cm)

1) Cut insulated lining and shade fabric as directed in cutting directions (page 61). Splice lining for added length, if necessary as directed on page 61. Position a 4" (10 cm) channel at lower edge of the shade, 8" (20.5) from cut edge.

2) Pin right sides of shade and insulated lining together with top and side edges even. The shade fabric will not lay flat because of the 3" (7.5 cm) added for side hem wrap. Stitch ½" (1.3 cm) seams. Zigzag or edgestitch close to cut edge to reduce bulk and prevent insulation from curling.

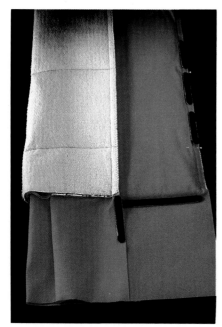

5) Place a 2½" (6.3 cm) strip of magnetic tape on the right side of shade fabric on the seam allowance of lower hem area, just below edge of insulation. If magnetic seal is used on lower edge, firmly press long strip of magnetic tape across shade at lower edge of insulation.

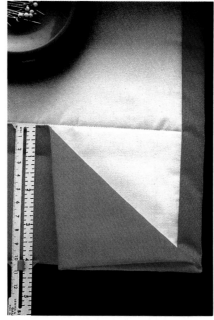

6) Turn shade right side out. Turn under 4" (10 cm) double-fold hem at lower edge. Be sure lower edge of shade is square. Adjust hem if necessary. Taper side hem edges slightly so they do not show on right side. Stitch close to hem fold on the channel stitching line.

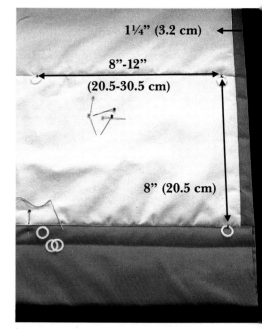

1¼" (3.2 cm)

8"-12"
(20.5-30.5 cm)

8" (20.5 cm)

7) Place shade, lining side up, on flat surface. Do not press. Mark positions for rings on quilting rows. Place rings 1¼" (3.2 cm) from sides. Space vertical rows 8" to 12" (20.5 to 30.5 cm) apart. Pin through all layers and each ring to prevent shifting. Tack on rings.

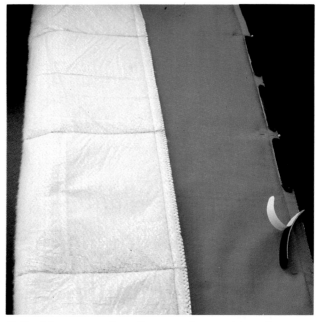

3) Place the roll of magnetic tape on newspaper and spray paint one edge of the roll. This marks the lengthwise polarity. The polarity is important when attaching magnets to shade and window. Separate scored lengths of magnets or cut 3¼" (8.3 cm) lengths. Round tape corners with scissors to prevent sharp corners from tearing fabric.

4) Position two strips of magnetic tape in each channel on the seam allowance on wrong side of shade fabric. Place all magnets in the same direction, using painted edges as guide to polarity. Peel off paper backing and press firmly. Do not place magnets in mounting ease at top of shade or lower hem area.

8) Wrap ends of weight rod with tape, or file rough edges to reduce wear on shade fabric. Insert weight rod in lower hem. Slipstitch opening closed.

9) Attach a plain or lock pulley for first row on the pulling side of shade. Pulley accommodates more strings than screw eyes and supports the additional weight. Attach weighted shade pull. Mount and string shade (page 64).

10) Clean surface with alcohol to insure a tight bond. Place long strips of magnetic tape on side edges of shade, matching polarity. Place shade against wall. Peel off paper backing; press to wall. Use rolling pin to remove air bubbles.

How to Mount an Insulated Shade Using an Outside Mount

1) Cut 1"×2" (2.5×5 cm) board to the width of finished shade. Wrap shade up and over narrow edge of board and staple to back (wide side). Place screw eyes directly above each row of rings.

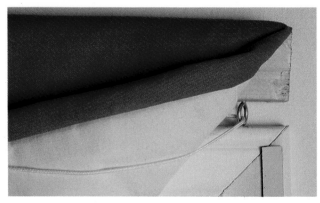

2) String as for Roman shade (pages 50 and 51, steps 14 and 15). Screw wide side of mounting board into wall. Attach awning cleat to side of window frame or wall if not using a lock pulley.

How to Mount an Insulated Shade Using an Inside Mount

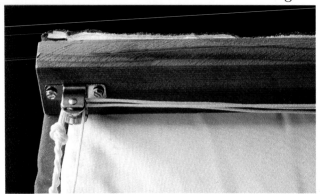

1) Cut 1"×2" (2.5×5 cm) board long enough to fit inside window opening. Wrap shade over narrow edge of board and staple. Place screw eyes directly above each row of rings. String as for Roman shade (pages 50 and 51, steps 14 and 15).

2) Screw wide edge of mounting board into top of window frame. Accuracy is important in fitting the shade. Additional molding may be necessary around inside of window frame for magnetic edge seal strips. Attach awning cleat if not using a lock pulley.

How to Mount an Insulated Shade Using a Hybrid Mount

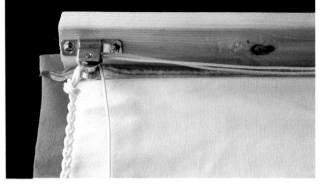

1) Cut 1"×2" (2.5×5 cm) board to fit inside window. Fold shade over at top on finished length line. Place right side of mounting flap on narrow edge of board so sides of shade extend equally beyond board and fold is along top edge of board.

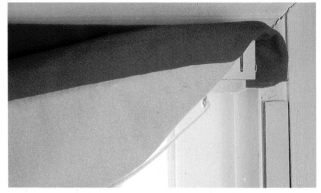

2) Anchor with staples. Staple narrow strip of cardboard on the shade; let shade fall forward over staples. Check for fit in window. Trim excess fabric below cardboard strip. String as for Roman shade (pages 50 and 51, steps 14 and 15). Screw mount board into top of window frame. Attach awning cleat.

Cornices & Valances

A shirred valance (shown above) is a short shirred curtain. Install a shirred valance on a separate rod that extends 1" to 2" (2.5 to 5 cm) in front of the curtain rod.

A flat or tailored valance has no extra fullness. This valance is installed on a plain curtain rod, or attached to a 1"×4" (2.5×10 cm) mounting board. Install the mounting board with angle irons to extend beyond the curtain; on Roman shades, attach the valance directly to the shade's mounting board.

Cornices and valances are decorative headings which are mounted above shades, curtains and draperies. Their functional purpose is to hide exposed rods, plain mountings and tops of conventionally mounted roller shades.

Cornices and valances are usually about one-eighth the curtain or shade length. Make cornices 3" to 4" (7.5 to 10 cm) wider than the window treatment, projecting 2" to 3" (5 to 7.5 cm) in front of it. With shades and curtains, cornices should fit close to the window molding; with draperies, extend the cornice beyond the molding to allow room for draperies to clear the window when they are pulled open.

Cornices are firm, box-like structures made from wood, heavy cardboard or foamboard. They are usually padded and upholstered, and may be cut in decorative shapes along the front edge.

Valances are simple fabric headings which do not have hard backings. Make them shirred or flat, with plain, trimmed or shaped edges to suit the window treatment.

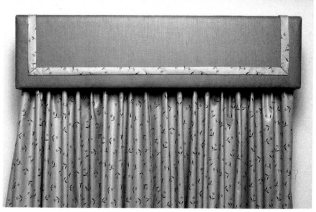

A padded cornice has a closed top which protects curtains from dust. Cornices also make windows more energy efficient by limiting airflow at the top of the window.

Pleated Draperies

Pleated draperies are easy to sew with pleater tape, which eliminates tedious, complicated measuring.

Pinch pleats are the traditional pleated heading for draperies. Each pleat is actually three small pleats grouped together at regular intervals. Pleater tape for pinch pleats has evenly spaced pockets woven into it; special four-pronged hooks inserted into the pockets draw up the pleats.

Select pleater tape that gives the desired drapery fullness. Some pleater tapes are designed to give an exact double fullness; others allow for more or less than double fullness, depending on how pockets are used. Determine drapery fullness according to the fabric weight; lightweight fabrics require more fullness than heavy fabrics.

Panel draperies are stationary pleated panels that hang at the sides of the window.

Draw draperies can be closed to cover the entire width of the window. These draperies hang on traverse rods and pull open to one side only (one-way draw) or to both sides (two-way draw).

Before cutting fabric or tape, prepleat the *tape only* using pleater hooks to determine the finished width of the drapes and pleat position. Pleat tape to the width of the drapery panel and hang it on the rod. Adjust pleats as necessary so the last pleat of the panel is at the corner of the rod return. Do not place pleats on the return or at the center of two-way draperies where panels overlap. Remove hooks and measure tape to determine finished width of drapery panels. (See steps 1 and 2.)

✂ Cutting Directions

After pleating tape to correct size, cut pleater tape for each panel so that similar panels have pockets in same position. Allow ½" (1.3 cm) at each end of tape for finishing.

Cut decorator fabric the width of the pleater tape, allowing 1" (2.5 cm) for each seam (if necessary) for joining fabric widths.

For draperies, cut width of fabric the length of tape plus 4" (10 cm) for 1" (2.5 cm) double-fold side hems; for length, cut fabric finished length, plus 6½" (16.5 cm) for 3" (7.5 cm) double-fold hem and ½" (1.3 cm) for turning under on upper edge.

YOU WILL NEED

Decorator fabric for draperies.

Pleater tape to match style of heading.

Pleater hooks and end pins.

How to Sew Unlined Pinch-pleat Draperies

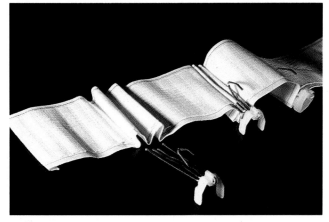

1) Prepleat pleater tape to finished width of drapery panel. Leave space unpleated at one end of tape for overlap in center of window, and at other end for return.

2) Position the pleater tape on installed traverse rod and adjust pleats if necessary. Fold ends under ½" (1.3 cm). Remove hooks. Cut panels using pleater tape as guide.

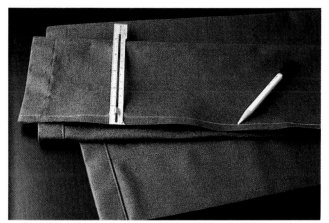

3) Finish drapery hems. Turn under 3" (7.5 cm) double-fold hem on lower edge and 1" (2.5 cm) double-fold hems on sides. Mark ½" (1.3 cm) from upper edge on right side of drapery.

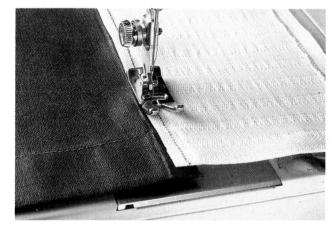

4) Pin upper edge of pleater tape, pocket side up, along marked line so that pleater tape overlaps drapery ½" (1.3 cm). Stitch ¼" (6 mm) from edge of pleater tape.

5) Fold sewn tape to inside of drapery so tape is even with top of drapery. Press. Stitch lower edge and both sides of tape, following guideline on tape, if marked.

6) Insert hooks. Push prongs all the way up into pleats, making sure tape is drawn to bottom of hook. Adjust folds between hooks.

Pillows

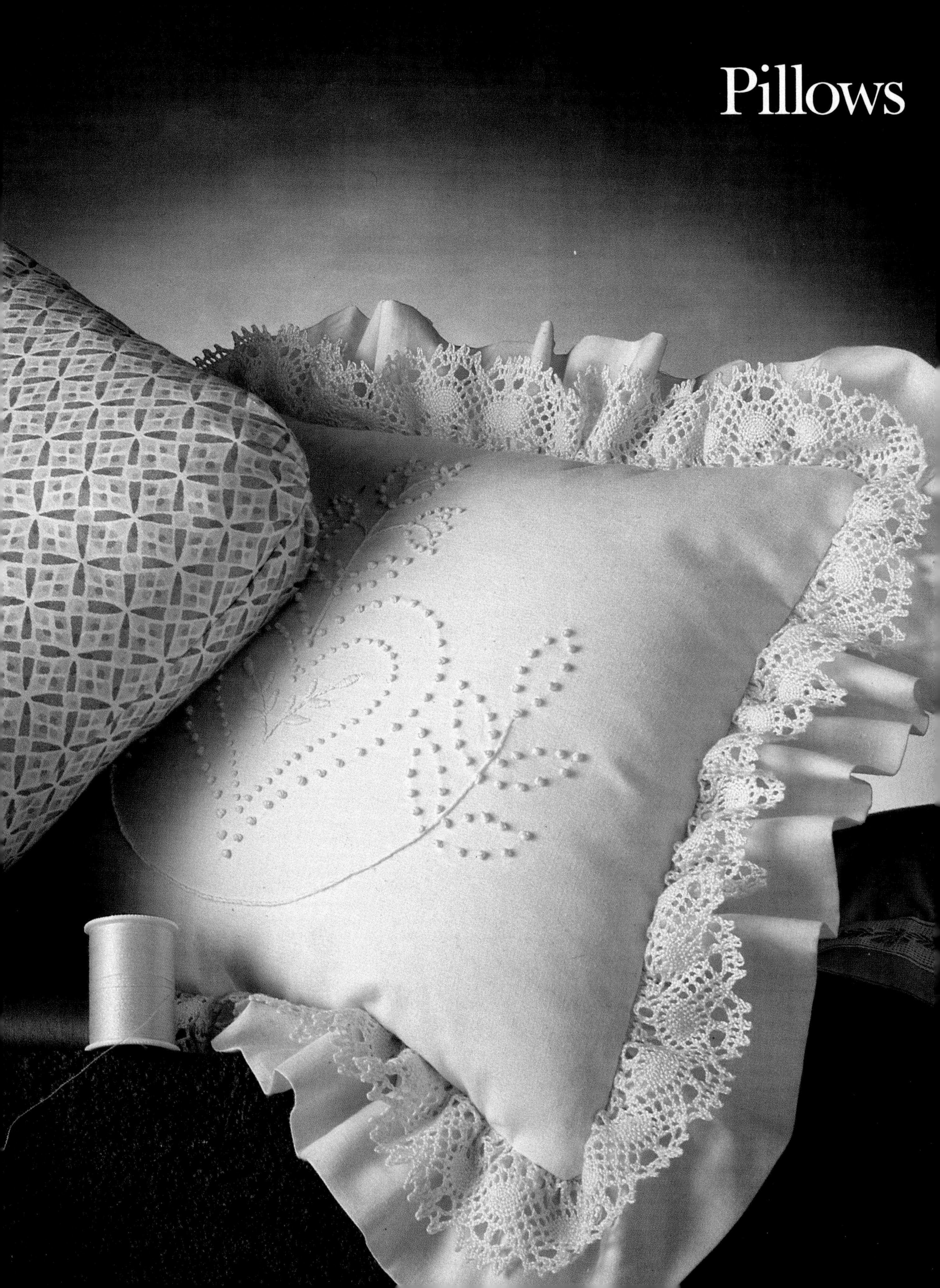

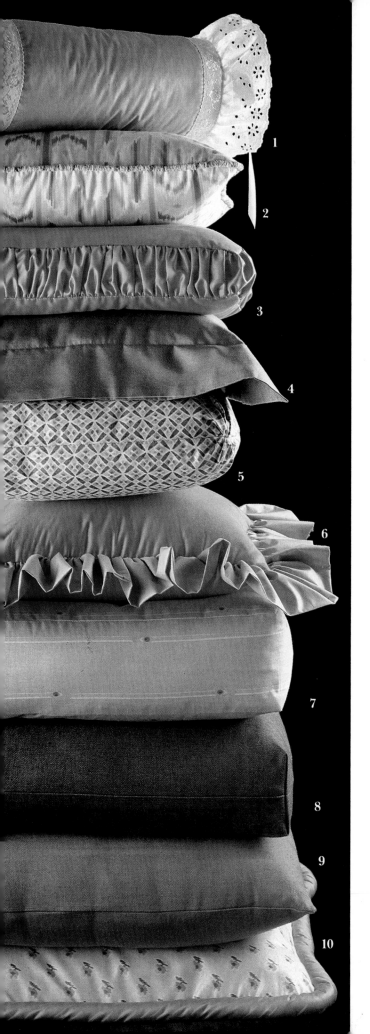

Pillow Fashions

Pillow styles range from simple to elaborate. Choice of technique affects your sewing time. Choose a simple knife-edge pillow, or invest more time in tailoring a box pillow complete with cording and a zipper.

1) Neckrolls are small round bolsters that are often trimmed with lace or ruffles. Sleeping bag pillows are the simplest neckroll bolsters to make. They are made with a drawstring closure at each end of a one-piece tube.

2) Shirred corded pillow is made by inserting gathered cording in the seam around the pillow. Cording is gathered using a technique, known as shirring, to gather the bias strip that covers the cord. Make cording in matching or contrasting fabric to add a decorative finish to a pillow.

3) Shirred box pillow uses shirring to gather both edges of the boxing strip. This makes the pillow softer than the traditional box pillow.

4) Flange pillow has a single or double, flat self-border, usually 2" (5 cm) wide, around a plump knife-edge pillow.

5) Mock box pillow is a variation of the knife-edge pillow, with shaped corners to add depth. Corners made using *gathered* style are tied inside the pillow.

6) Ruffled pillow features gathered lace or ruffles made in single or double layers. Pillow tops framed by ruffles in matching or contrasting fabric make attractive showcases for needlepoint, quilting, embroidery or candlewicking.

7) Box pillow has the added depth of a straight or shirred boxing strip. It can be soft for a scatter pillow, or firm for a chair cushion or floor pillow.

8) Mock box pillow can be made with *mitered* corners to create a tailored box shape.

9) Knife-edge pillow is the easiest pillow to make. It consists of two pieces of fabric sewn together, turned right side out and stuffed.

10) Corded pillow is a knife-edge pillow with matching or contrasting cording sewn in the seams. Use purchased cording or make your own. Or finish the pillow with a mock corded edge for a corded look without extra sewing time or fabric. Corded pillows are often called piped pillows.

Pillow Fabrics, Forms & Fillings

To choose the right fabric for your pillow, consider how the pillow will be used and where it will be placed in your home. For a pillow that will receive hard wear, select a sturdy, firmly woven fabric that will retain its shape.

Pillows get their shape from forms or loose fillings. Depending on their washability, loose fillings may be stuffed directly into the pillow covering or encased in a separate liner for easy removal. For ease in laundering or dry cleaning, make a separate inner covering or liner for the stuffing, using lightweight muslin or lining fabric, or use purchased pillow forms. Make the liner as you would a knife-edge pillow (pages 72 and 73), fill it with stuffing, and machine-stitch it closed. Choose from several kinds of forms and fillings.

Standard polyester forms are square, round and rectangular for knife-edge pillows in sizes from 10" to 30" (25.5 to 76 cm). These forms are nonallergenic, washable, do not bunch, and may have muslin or polyester outer coverings. Choose muslin-covered forms for pillows with hook and loop tape closings. The loose muslin fibers do not catch on the rough side of the tape.

Polyurethane foam is available in sheets ½" to 5" (1.3 to 12.5 cm) thick for firm pillows and cushions. Some stores carry a high-density foam, 4" (10 cm) thick, for extra firm cushions. Since cutting the foam is difficult, ask the salesperson to cut a piece to the size of your pillow. If you must cut your own foam, use an electric or serrated knife with silicone lubricant sprayed on the blade. Polyurethane foam is also available shredded.

Polyester fiberfill is washable, nonallergenic filling for pillows or pillow liners. Fiberfill comes in loose-pack bags or pressed into batting sheets of varying densities. For a smooth pillow, sew an inner liner of batting, then stuff with loose fill. Soften the hard edges of polyurethane foam by wrapping the form with batting.

Kapok is vegetable fiber filling, favored by some decorators because of its softness. However, kapok is messy to work with and becomes matted with use.

Down is washed, quill-less feathers from the breasts of geese and ducks. Down makes the most luxurious pillows, but it is expensive and not readily available.

Knife-edge
Pillow or Liner

Knife-edge pillows are plump in the center and flat around the edges. These simple pillows can be made in half an hour with less than half a yard (.50 m) of fabric.

Use the knife-edge pillow directions to make removable pillow liners. Sew liners from muslin, sheeting, cotton sateen or similar fabrics.

✄ Cutting Directions

Cut front and back 1" (2.5 cm) larger than finished pillow or liner. If inserting a centered zipper in pillow back, cut back 1½" (3.8 cm) wider than front.

YOU WILL NEED

Decorator fabric or liner fabric for pillow front and back.

Lining fabric for pillow liner, front and back.

Pillow form or polyester fiberfill. Use 8 to 12 oz. (227 to 360 g) fiberfill for a 14" (35.5 cm) pillow, depending on desired firmness.

Zipper or other closure (optional) may be inserted (pages 88 to 91).

How to Make a Knife-edge Pillow or Liner

1) Fold front into fourths. Mark a point halfway between the corner and the fold on each open side. At corner, mark a point ½" (1.3 cm) from each raw edge.

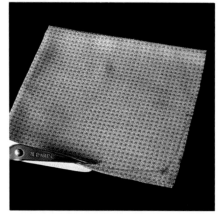

2) Trim from center mark to corner, gradually tapering from the edge to the ½" (1.3 cm) mark. Taper from ½" (1.3 cm) mark to center mark on opposite edge.

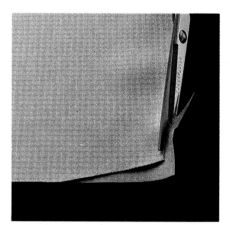

3) Unfold front and use it as a pattern for trimming back so that all corners are slightly rounded. This will eliminate dog ears on the corners of the finished pillow.

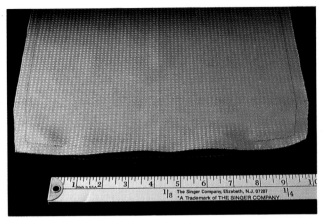

4) Pin front to back, right sides together. Stitch ½" (1.3 cm) seam, leaving 8" (20.5 cm) opening on one side for turning and stuffing. Backstitch at the beginning and end of seam.

5) Trim corners diagonally, ⅛" (3 mm) from stitching. On pillows with curved edges or round corners, clip seam allowance to stitching at intervals along curves to ease seam for turning.

6) Turn pillow right side out, pulling out corners. Press seams smooth. Press under the back seam allowance in opening.

7) Insert a purchased pillow form into the pillow, or stuff the pillow with polyester fiberfill as in step 8. Use a removable form or liner in pillows that will be dry cleaned or laundered.

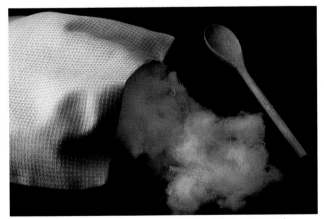

8) Stuff pillow or liner with polyester fiberfill, gently pulling pieces apart to fluff and separate fibers. Work stuffing into corners with long, blunt tool such as a spoon handle.

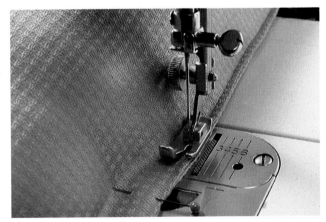

9) Pin opening closed and edgestitch on folded edge, backstitching at beginning and end of stitching line; or slipstitch by hand.

Corded Knife-edge Pillow

Cording adds stablilty to pillows and gives them a more tailored look. Cording is made by covering cord with bias strips.

✂ Cutting Directions

Cut pillow front and back 1" (2.5 cm) larger than finished pillow. If inserting a centered zipper, cut back 1½" (3.8 cm) wider than front. Cut bias strips for cording as directed in step 1.

YOU WILL NEED

Decorator fabric for pillow front, back and cording.

Cord (twisted white cotton or polyester cable), 3" (7.5 cm) longer than distance around pillow.

Pillow form or knife-edge liner.

Zipper or other closure (optional) may be inserted (pages 88 to 91).

How to Make a Corded Knife-edge Pillow

Fold

a

b

c

1) Cut bias strips. Locate bias line by folding fabric diagonally so selvage aligns with crosswise cut. For ¼" (6 mm) cord, mark off and cut 1⅝" (4.2 cm) strips parallel to bias line. Cut wider strips for thicker cord. Stop cutting when last strip is still on crosswise cut. Strips are easier to join if ends are on crosswise grain.

2) Pin strips at right angles, right sides together, offset slightly **(a)**. Stitch ¼" (6 mm) seams **(b)**, and press open, making one continuous strip equal in length to perimeter of pillow plus 3" (7.5 cm). Trim points of seams even with edges **(c)**.

3) Center cord on wrong side of bias strip. Fold strip over cord, aligning raw edges. Using zipper foot on right side of needle, machine-baste close to cord, gently stretching bias to help cording lie smoothly around pillow.

4) Pin cording to right side of pillow front, cording toward center, raw edges aligned. To ease corners, clip bastestitching to seam allowances at corners.

5) Stitch on bastestitching line. Stop stitching 2" (5 cm) from point where cording ends will meet. Leave needle in fabric. Cut off one end of cording so it overlaps the other end by 1" (2.5 cm).

6) Take out 1" (2.5 cm) of stitching from each end of cording. Trim cord ends so they just meet.

7) Fold under ½" (1.3 cm) of overlapping bias strip. Lap it around the other end and finish stitching. Pin pillow front to back, right sides together.

8) Place pillow edge under needle with front on top. Using zipper foot, stitch inside bastestitching line; crowd stitching against cord. Leave 8" (20.5 cm) opening. Finish as for knife-edge pillow (page 73, steps 7 to 9).

Mock Box Pillow

Mock box pillows are variations of knife-edge pillows and can be made in three different styles. Mitered pillows have a short seam across each corner to create a tailored box shape. Corners on gathered styles are tied inside the pillow. Pleated pillows have neat tucks at each corner. The term Turkish or harem pillow may refer to either the gathered or the pleated pillow style.

✄ Cutting Directions

Cut pillow front and back the size of finished pillow plus the depth measurement plus 1" (2.5 cm) for seams. For example, for a 14" (35.5 cm) pillow, 3" (7.5 cm) deep, cut front and back 18" (46 cm) square.

YOU WILL NEED

Knife-edge pillow form, 2" (5 cm) larger than pillow. Or, make a mock box pillow liner using the following directions.

Decorator fabric for pillow front and back.

Zipper or other closure (optional) may be inserted in seam (page 91).

How to Make a Mock Box Pillow with Mitered Corners

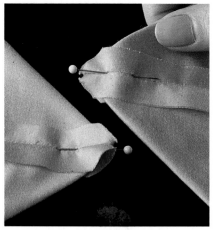

1) Stitch as directed (page 73, step 4). Press seams open. Separate front and back at corners. Center seams on each side of corner, on top of each other. Pin through seam.

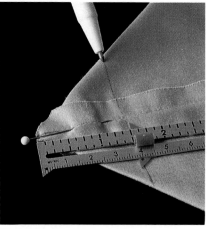

2) Measure on side seam from corner to half the finished depth; for example, for pillow 3" (7.5 cm) deep, measure 1½" (3.8 cm) from corner. Draw a line perpendicular to the seam.

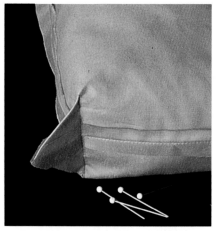

3) Stitch across corner of pillow on marked line, backstitching at beginning and end. Do not trim seam. Finish as for knife-edge pillow (page 73, steps 6 to 9).

How to Make a Mock Box Pillow with Gathered Corners

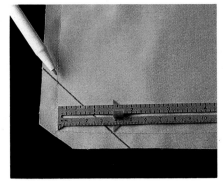

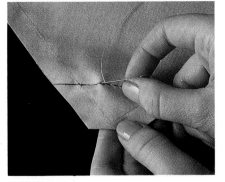

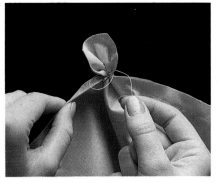

1) Stitch front to back as for knife-edge pillow (page 73, step 4). Measure on each seam line from corner point to half the finished pillow depth. Connect corner points with diagonal line.

2) Hand-baste on diagonal line with topstitching and buttonhole twist or doubled thread. Pull up thread to gather.

3) Wrap thread several times around gathered corner; secure with tight knot. Do not trim corner. Repeat for each corner. Finish as for knife-edge pillow (page 73, steps 6 to 9).

How to Make a Mock Box Pillow with Pleated Corners

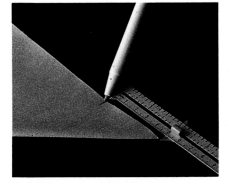

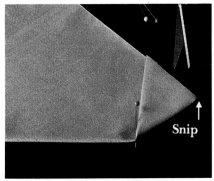

Snip

1) Fold corner in half diagonally. On cut edge, measure from corner to half the finished pillow depth plus ½" (1.3 cm); for example, for pillow 3" (7.5 cm) deep, measure 2" (5 cm) from corner point.

2) Mark measured point with ¼" (6 mm) snips through both seam allowances. Fold corner back at snips to form triangle. Mark fold with pin. Press triangle in place.

3) Spread corner flat, right side up. Fold fabric from snip to pin; bring fold to pressed center mark, forming pleat. Pin pleat in place. Repeat for other side.

4) Baste across pleat, ½" (1.3 cm) from raw edge, removing pins as you stitch. Trim triangle-shaped piece from corner. Repeat for each corner of front and back.

5) Pin front to back, right sides together, with front tucked into back to form a "basket." Match pleated corners precisely.

6) Stitch ½" (1.3 cm) seam. Finish as for knife-edge pillow (page 73, steps 6 to 9).

Mock Corded Pillow

The mock corded pillow is a basic knife-edge pillow with cording sewn around the edges *after* the pillow is assembled.

✂ Cutting Directions

Cut pillow front 1" (2.5 cm) larger than finished pillow. Cut back the same length as front, and 1½" (3.8 cm) wider for closure seam.

YOU WILL NEED

Decorator fabric for pillow front and back.

Hook and loop tape or zipper, 2" (5 cm) shorter than length of pillow back. Closures must be inserted in center of pillow back.

Cord, [½" (1.3 cm) welt cording or clothesline], equal in length to distance around pillow.

Pillow form or knife-edge liner.

How to Make a Mock Corded Pillow

1) Trim corners of front and back into gentle curves. Insert hook and loop tape or other closure in center of pillow back (pages 89 and 90).

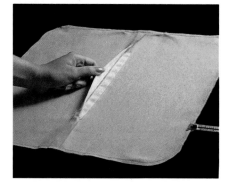

2) Pin front to back, right sides together. Stitch ¼" (6 mm) seam around entire pillow. Turn pillow right side out.

3) Pin cord inside pillow, as tightly as possible against outer seam. Ends of cord should just meet.

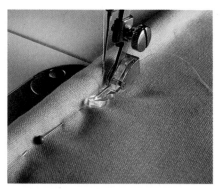

4) Stitch cord from right side, crowding stitching against cord, using zipper foot. Leave 3" (7.5 cm) opening where cord ends meet.

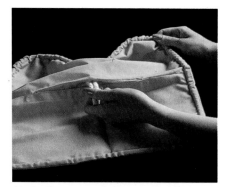

5) Pull out cord about 4" (10 cm) at each end to gather corners. Adjust gathers. Cut cord so ends just meet. Tack ends together.

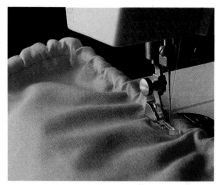

6) Topstitch opening closed, using zipper foot. Start and end stitching on previous stitching lines. Insert pillow form or liner.

Box Pillow

Use box pillows as cushions as well as for casual pillows. Box pillows are firm because of the boxing strip that is sewn between the pillow's front and back.

✂ Cutting Directions

Cut pillow front and back 1" (2.5 cm) larger than finished pillow. Also cut boxing strip with length equal to distance around pillow plus 1" (2.5 cm) for seams, width equal to depth of pillow plus 1" (2.5 cm).

YOU WILL NEED

Decorator fabric for pillow front, back and boxing strip.

Pillow form or knife-edge liner, 2" to 3" (5 to 7.5 cm) larger than finished pillow.

How to Make a Box Pillow

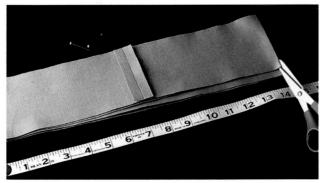

1) Stitch short ends of boxing strip, right sides together, to form continuous loop. Fold loop into fourths and mark each fold with ⅜" (1 cm) clip on both edges.

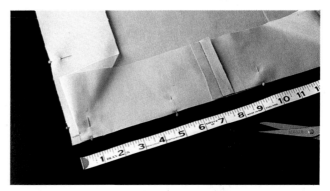

2) Pin boxing strip to pillow front, right sides together, raw edges even, matching clipped points on strip to pillow corners.

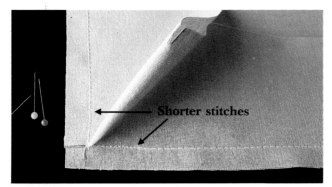

Shorter stitches

3) Stitch ½" (1.3 cm) seam, shortening stitches 1" (2.5 cm) on each side of corner and taking one or two stitches diagonally across each corner instead of sharp pivot. This reinforces corners and makes a neater point.

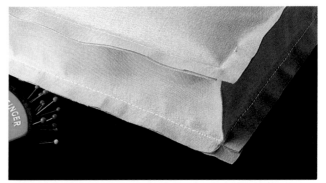

4) Pin boxing strip to pillow back, right sides together, matching clipped points to pillow corners. Stitch ½" (1.3 cm) seam as in step 3, leaving one side open to insert form. Finish as for knife-edge pillow (page 73, steps 6 to 9).

Ruffled Pillow

Ruffles add interest to a pillow or enhance fine needlework pillows. Make ruffles from matching or contrasting fabric or from purchased lace or eyelet ruffling.

✂ Cutting Directions

Cut pillow front and back 1" (2.5 cm) larger than finished pillow. Cut ruffle strips twice the desired width plus 1" (2.5 cm) for seam, length two to three times the distance around pillow; cut on crosswise grain. Ruffles are usually about 3" (7.5 cm) wide.

YOU WILL NEED

Decorator fabric for pillow front and back and double ruffle.

Purchased ruffling (optional), equal in length to distance around pillow plus 1" (2.5 cm).

Cord, (string, crochet cotton or dental floss) for gathering.

Pillow form or knife-edge liner.

How to Make a Ruffled Pillow

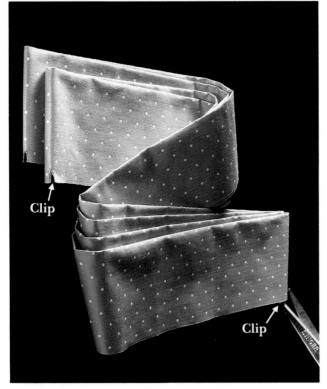

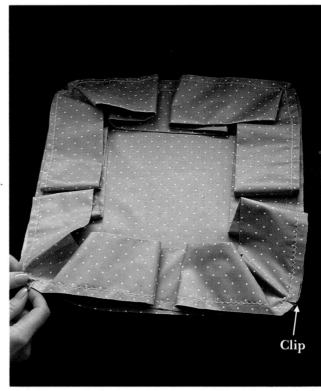

1) Join short ends of ruffle strip to form a continuous loop. Fold strip in half lengthwise, wrong sides together. Fold ruffle loop into fourths. Mark each fold with a ⅜" (1 cm) clip.

2) Prepare raw edge for gathering (page 38). Match clips on ruffle to corners on right side of pillow front. Pin at corners with raw edges even.

3) Pull up the gathering cord until ruffle fits each side of the pillow front. Distribute gathers evenly and pin ruffle in place.

4) Machine-baste ruffle to pillow front, stitching just inside gathering row.

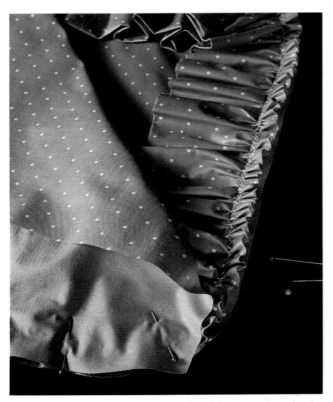

5) Pin pillow back to front, right sides together, with ruffle between pieces. Stitch ½" (1.3 cm) seam, leaving 8" (20.5 cm) opening on one side for turning.

6) Turn pillow right side out. Insert pillow form or knife-edge liner and slipstitch opening closed.

Flange Pillows

A *flange* is a flat self-border around a plump knife-edge pillow. It may be single or double, and is usually about 2" (5 cm) wide. The double flange pillow is made with a zipper or other closure; the single flange pillow is sewn closed.

✂ Cutting Directions

For single flange, cut pillow front and back 5" (12.5 cm) larger than stuffed inner area. This allows for 2" (5 cm) flange and ½" (1.3 cm) seam on each side.

For double flange, cut pillow front 9" (23 cm) larger than pillow form. This allows for 2" (5 cm) flange and ½" (1.3 cm) seam on each side. Cut pillow back 1½" (3.8 cm) wider than front for closure.

YOU WILL NEED

Decorator fabric for pillow front and back.

Polyester fiberfill for single flange pillow, about 6 oz. (170 g) for 12" (30.5 cm) pillow.

Pillow form or knife-edge liner for double flange pillow, to fit inner area.

Zipper or alternate closure for double flange pillow, 2" (5 cm) shorter than length of stuffed inner area (pages 89 and 90).

How to Make a Single-Flange Pillow

1) Pin right sides of pillow together. Stitch ½" (1.3 cm) seam, leaving 8" (20.5 cm) opening. Turn right side out. Press. Topstitch 2" (5 cm) from edge, beginning and ending at opening.

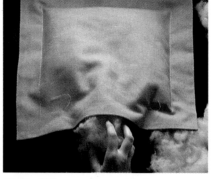

2) Stuff inner area with loose polyester fiberfill, making sure stuffing gets into corners. Do not stuff flange (border area).

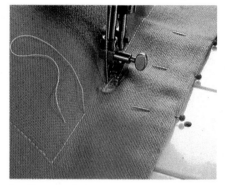

3) Topstitch inner area closed, using zipper foot, starting and ending at first stitching line. Slipstitch flange closed, or edgestitch around entire pillow.

How to Make a Double-Flange Pillow with Mitered Corners

1) Insert zipper (page 90), hook and loop tape or snap tape (page 89) in pillow back.

2) Press under 2½" (6.3 cm) on each side of front and back. Place front and back together to make sure corners match; adjust pressed folds if necessary.

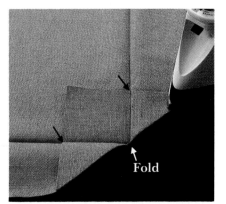

3) Open out corner. Fold corner back diagonally so pressed fold lines match (arrows). Press diagonal fold.

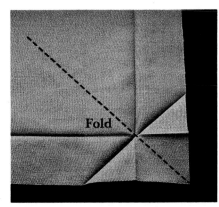

4) Open out corner. Fold through center of corner (dotted line), right sides together.

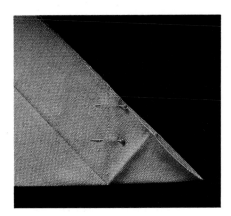

5) Pin on diagonal fold line, raw edges even. Stitch on fold line at right angle to corner fold.

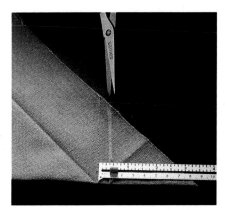

6) Trim seam to ⅜" (1 cm). Press seam open.

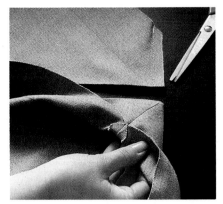

7) Turn corner right side out. Use point turner or blunt end of scissors to get a sharp point. Press edges. Repeat with other corners, front and back.

8) Pin pillow front to back, wrong sides together, matching mitered corners carefully.

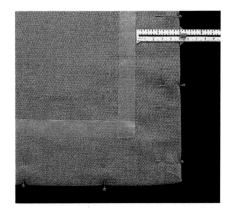

9) Measure 2" (5 cm) from edge for flange; mark stitching line with transparent tape. Topstitch through all thicknesses along edge of tape. Insert pillow form or liner.

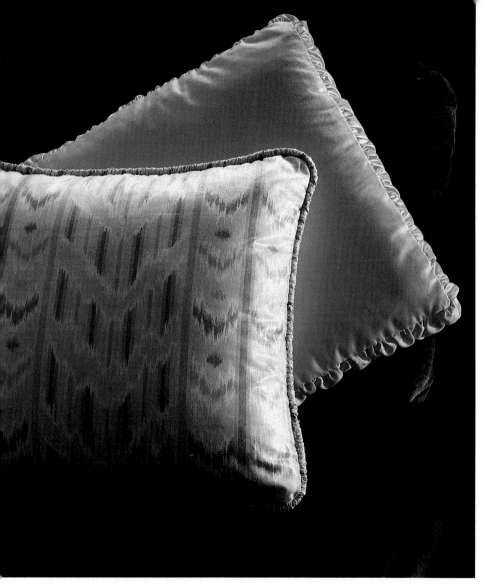

Shirred Pillows

Shirred cording or boxing strips give pillows a formal look.

✂ Cutting Directions

For shirred box pillow, cut pillow front and back 1" (2.5 cm) larger than finished pillow. Cut boxing strip 1" (2.5 cm) wider than depth of form and two to three times longer than distance around form.

For shirred corded pillow, cut pillow front and back 1" (2.5 cm) larger than finished pillow. For cording, cut fabric strips on crosswise grain, wide enough to cover cord plus 1" (2.5 cm) for seam. The combined length of the strips should be two to three times the distance around pillow.

YOU WILL NEED

Decorator fabric for pillow front and back and for cording or boxing strips.

Cord (twisted white cotton or polyester cable, if making shirred cording). Cut 3" (7.5 cm) longer than distance around pillow.

Gathering cord (string, crochet cotton or dental floss).

Pillow form or knife-edge liner wrapped in polyester batting.

How to Make a Shirred Box Pillow

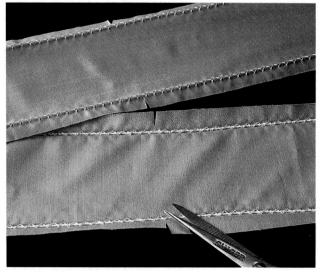

1) Sew the gathering rows along the upper and lower edges of the boxing strip by zigzagging over the gathering cord. Fold boxing strip into fourths and mark both edges of folds with ⅜" (1 cm) clips.

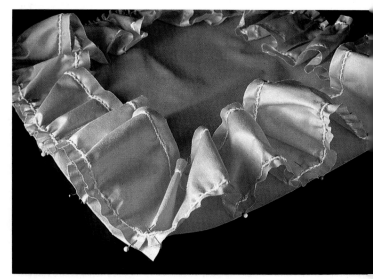

2) Pin boxing strip to pillow front, right sides together, raw edges even, matching clips on boxing strip to pillow corners. Pull up the gathering cord to fit each side of the pillow.

How to Make Shirred Cording

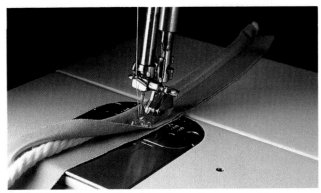

1) Join ends of cording strips using ¼" (6 mm) seams. Press the seams open. Stitch one end of the cord to the wrong side of the cording strip, ⅜" (1 cm) from the end of the strip.

2) Fold cording strip around cord, wrong sides together, matching raw edges. Using zipper foot, machine-baste for 6" (15 cm), close to but not crowding cord. Stop stitching with needle in fabric.

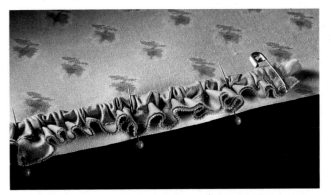

3) Raise presser foot. While gently pulling cord, push cording strip back to end of cord until fabric behind needle is tightly shirred. Continue stitching in 6" (15 cm) intervals until all cording is shirred.

4) Insert pin through strip and cord at end to prevent cord from sliding into cording strip. Attach shirred cording to pillow front and join ends of cord as for corded pillow, (page 75, steps 4 to 8).

3) Distribute gathers evenly, pinning as necessary. Stitch all four sides inside gathering row, stitching corners as directed on page 79, step 3.

4) Pin the lower edge of the boxing strip to pillow back. Repeat steps 2 and 3, except stitch only three sides, leaving one side open to insert the pillow form.

5) Finish as for knife-edge pillow, (page 73, steps 6 to 9), substituting a pillow form wrapped in polyester batting for stuffing.

Neckroll & Sleeping Bag Pillow

Neckrolls and sleeping bag pillows are small, round bolsters with removable covers that gather at the ends with drawstrings.

✂ Cutting Directions

For neckroll, cut fabric same width as circumference of pillow plus 1" (2.5 cm) for seam; length equal to length of pillow plus 1" (2.5 cm). Cut two end strips, same length as circumference of pillow plus 1" (2.5 cm) for seam; width same as pillow radius plus 1½" (3.8 cm).

For sleeping bag pillow, cut fabric same width as circumference of pillow plus 1" (2.5 cm); length equal to length of pillow plus diameter of pillow plus 1½" (3.8 cm) for casing.

YOU WILL NEED

Decorator fabric for tube, and for two end strips if making neckroll.

Ruffled eyelet trim for neckroll. Cut two pieces, each same length as circumference of pillow plus 1" (2.5 cm) for seam.

Ribbon for drawstring, ¼" (6 mm) wide and about 1½ yards (1.4 m) long.

Polyester fiberfill batting to form pillow; width same as length of pillow, and about 1 yd. (.95 m) long.

How to Make a Neckroll

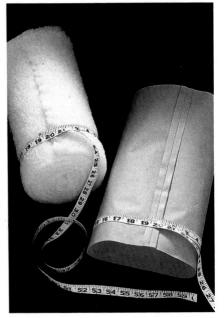

1) Roll batting as directed in step 1 for sleeping bag pillow. Fold fabric for tube in half lengthwise, right sides together. Stitch ½" (1.3 cm) seam on lengthwise edge; press seam open.

2) Turn tube right side out. Join ends of each strip of eyelet with French seams. Pin eyelet to each end of tube, right sides together, edges even. Stitch scant ½" (1.3 cm) seam.

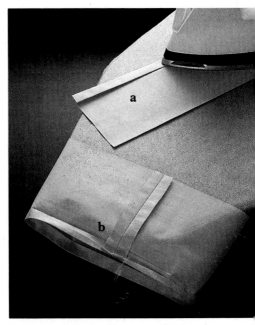

3) Press under ¼" (6 mm), then ½" (1.3 cm) on one long edge of each strip (a) to form casing for ribbon. Open pressed casing (b); stitch short ends of each strip, right sides together. Press seam open.

How to Make a Sleeping Bag Pillow

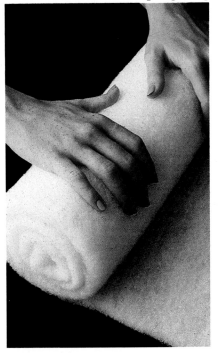

1) Roll up short side of polyester batting loosely until desired size for pillow. Tack end to roll with loose slipstitches. If using pillow form, wrap polyester batting around form twice; slipstitch to hold.

2) Press under ¼" (6 mm), then ½" (1.3 cm) on each end of fabric to form casing. Fold fabric in half lengthwise, right sides together. Stitch ½" (1.3 cm) seam on lengthwise edge; press seam open.

3) Stitch close to inside fold, starting and ending at seam. Backstitch to secure stitching. Finish pillow as directed in step 6 for neckroll.

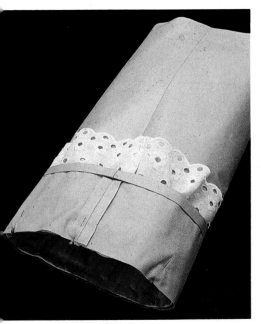

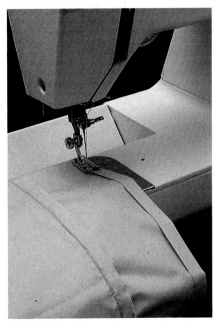

4) Pin unpressed edge of strips to ends of tube, right sides together, sandwiching eyelet between tube and strip. Stitch ½" (1.3 cm) seam. If machine has free arm, slip tube over arm to stitch circle.

5) Edgestitch close to inside folds of fabric strips, starting and ending at seam. Backstitch to secure stitching. Clip 3 or 4 stitches on casing seam to make opening for ribbon.

6) Thread ribbon through casings, using bodkin or safety pin. Clip ends of ribbon diagonally to prevent fraying. Insert rolled batting or form. Pull up ribbons and tie.

Pillow Closures

Zippers may be inserted in the pillow center back or side seam with a lapped or centered application. Although zippers are traditional pillow closures, there are several good alternatives.

A simple overlap closure is a technique for pillow shams (page 118) as well as an easy and inexpensive closure method for any pillow.

Snap tape and hook and loop (or self-gripping fastener) tape such as Velcro® are easy to handle and give closures a flat, smooth finish. Snap tape allows some give on closures and is suitable for pillows that are very soft.

How to Sew an Overlap Closure

1) Cut pillow back 4" to 5½" (10 to 14 cm) wider than front to allow 1½" to 3" (3.8 to 7.5 cm) overlap. Cut back in half, cutting *across* widened dimension.

2) Press under ¼" (6 mm), then 1" (2.5 cm) for double-fold hem on each center edge of pillow back. Blindstitch or edgestitch the hems in place.

3) Pin pillow front to back with raw edges even and hemmed edges overlapping in center. Stitch ½" (1.3 cm) seams. Turn right side out and insert pillow form or liner.

How to Sew a Pillow Closure with Hook and Loop or Snap Tape

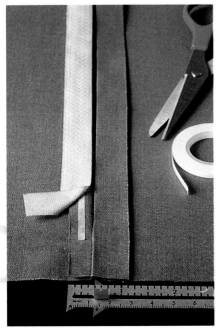

1) Prepare seam as for zipper (page 90). Cut hook and loop tape 1" (2.5 cm) longer than opening. Trim ¼" (6 mm) from one seam allowance. Place hook side of tape along fold of trimmed seam allowance so tape extends ½" (1.3 cm) beyond opening at each end. Pin, glue or baste.

2) Stitch hook side of tape close to edges on all four sides, stitching through pillow back and seam allowance. Stitches show on right side of pillow.

3) Stitch loop side of tape to wrong side of opposite seam allowance, overlapping tape ⅛" (3 mm) on seam allowance, and extending tape ½" (1.3 cm) beyond opening at each end.

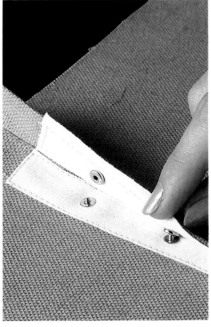

4) Turn loop side of tape to right side of seam allowance and stitch to seam allowance on remaining three sides.

5) Place hook side of tape on loop side of tape. Pin pillow front to back along three sides, right sides together. Stitch ½" (1.3 cm) seams. Turn pillow right side out and insert pillow form or liner.

6) Apply snap tape as directed in steps 1 to 5 making sure balls and sockets are aligned for smooth closure. Use zipper foot to stitch close to snaps.

How to Insert a Centered Zipper in a Pillow Back

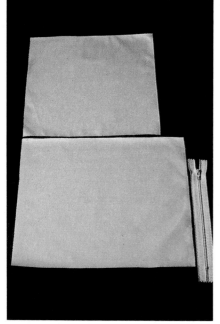

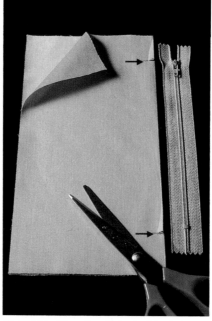

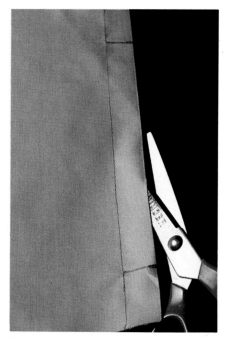

1) Cut pillow back 1½" (3.8 cm) wider than pillow front for a ¾" (2 cm) seam allowance. Use a zipper 2" (5 cm) shorter than length of pillow back.

2) Fold pillow back in half lengthwise, right sides together. Press. Center zipper along fold, leaving equal distance at each end. Snip into fold to mark ends of zipper coil (arrows).

3) Stitch ¾" (2 cm) seam from pillow edge to first snip. Backstitch. Machine-baste ½" (1.3 cm) past second snip. Shorten stitch length. Backstitch. Stitch to edge. Cut on fold; press seam open.

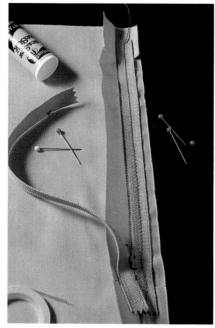

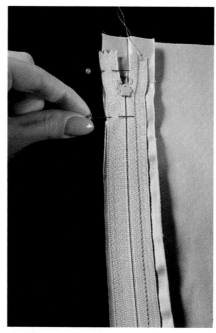

4) Open zipper and center it face down between snips with coil on seamline. Pin, glue or use basting tape to hold right side of zipper tape on right seam allowance. Machine-baste in place.

5) Close zipper and pin, glue or use basting tape to hold left side of tape to left seam allowance. Machine-baste in place.

6) Spread pillow flat, right side up. Mark zipper top and bottom with pins. Center ¾" (2 cm) transparent tape over seam as stitching guide. Topstitch around tape. Tie threads on wrong sides. Remove basting.

How to Insert a Lapped Zipper in a Pillow Seam

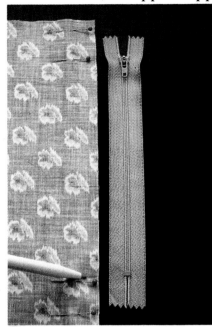

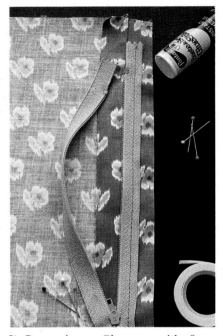

1) Use zipper 2" (5 cm) shorter than length of pillow. Pin pillow front to back along one side, right sides together. Position zipper along pinned seam, leaving equal distance at each edge. Mark ends of zipper coil on seam.

2) Stitch ¾" (2 cm) seam at each end of zipper opening; backstitch at marks. Press under ¾" (2 cm) seam allowance on pillow back.

3) Open zipper. Place one side face down on seam allowance of pillow front, coil on seamline. (Place coil on top of welt if pillow is corded). Pin, glue or baste in place. Using zipper foot, stitch tape to seam allowance only.

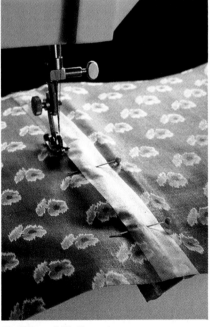

4) Close zipper. Spread pillow flat, right side up, making sure pressed seam allowance is over zipper coil. Pin the zipper in place from right side, catching the zipper tape underneath.

5) Place ⅜" (1 cm) transparent tape along seamline as stitching guide. Starting at seamline, stitch across bottom of zipper. Pivot and continue stitching. At top of zipper, pivot and stitch to seamline. Pull threads to wrong side and tie.

6) Open zipper. Turn pillow wrong side out and pin front to back on remaining three sides. Stitch ½" (1.3 cm) seam. Turn pillow right side out, insert pillow form or liner and zip closed.

Cushions

A cushion is usually shaped to fit a chair or bench. It has a firm inner core, and is anchored to furniture with a tie or tab. Follow the directions for any of the basic knife-edge or box pillows to make a cushion.

Because a cushion needs body, use a 1" (2.5 cm) thick piece of polyurethane wrapped with polyester batting to soften the edges, as a core for the cushion.

✂ Cutting Directions

For knife-edge cushion, cut front and back same size as area to be covered adding half the cushion depth and ½" (1.3 cm) for seams to each of the dimensions.

For box cushion, cut boxing strip desired width plus 1" (2.5 cm); cut front and back same size as area to be covered, adding 1" (2.5 cm) to each dimension for cushion fullness and ½" (1.3 cm) for seams.

How to Cut Fabric for Cushions

1) **Measure** length and width of area to be covered by cushion. For a square or rectangular cushion, use these dimensions to cut fabric. For a cushion with unusual shape, prepare a paper pattern.

2) **Cut** paper pattern in same shape as area to be covered. Mark the paper pattern to show where ties or tabs should be attached.

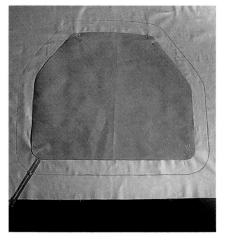

3) **Use** paper pattern to cut fabric for cushion, adding amount for depth and seams for cushion style. Transfer tie or tab markings to edge of right side of fabric.

Tufted Cushion

Add button tufting to chair or bench cushions to prevent filling from shifting inside the cover. Tufting is done after the cushion is finished. Tufted cushion covers are usually not removed, so zippers or other closures are not necessary.

Use covered flat buttons with a shank. Buttons for covering are available in kits, complete with a button front and back, and tools that simplify covering the button. Dampen the button fabric just before beginning. As the fabric dries around the button, it will shrink slightly to fit smoothly.

YOU WILL NEED

Long needle, with large eye.

Strong thread such as button and carpet thread or buttonhole twist.

Flat dressmaker buttons with shanks, two for each tuft.

How to Tuft a Cushion

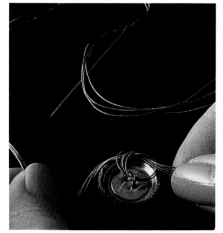

1) Thread a long needle, with extra-strong button and carpet thread or several strands of buttonhole twist. Thread strands through button shank; tie ends to shank with double knot.

2) Push needle through cushion, pulling button tight against pillow to create a "dimple." Clip thread near needle.

3) Thread second button on one strand of thread. Tie single knot with both strands and pull until button is tight against bottom of cushion. Wrap thread two or three times around button shank. Tie double knot. Trim threads.

Cushion Ties

Attach cushions to chairs with traditional fabric ties. Ties prevent cushions from sliding, and add a decorative accent to chairs.

Make ties to suit the style of the chair and cushion. Experiment with different sized fabric strips tied around the chair posts, to determine the appropriate length and width of the ties. Trim the fabric strip to desired size to use as a pattern.

✂ Cutting Directions
Cut each tie 1½" (3.8 cm) longer and 1" (2.5 cm) wider than the fabric pattern, allowing ½" (1.3 cm) for seam end and 1" (2.5 cm) for knotting the finished end. Cut two ties for each post where the ties will be attached.

How to Make Cushion Ties

1) Make two ties for each post where ties will be attached. Press under ¼" (6 mm) on long edges of each tie. Press tie in half lengthwise, wrong sides together, pressed edges even; pin.

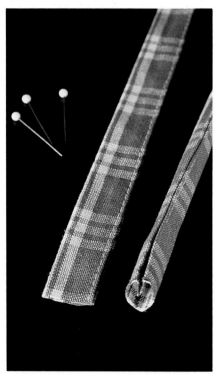

2) Edgestitch along open edge of ties. Leave both ends of tie open. Tie a single knot at one end of tie, enclosing the raw edges in the knot.

3) Pin unfinished ends of ties to right side of cushion front at marks. Pin cushion front to back, right sides together. Stitch, backstitching over ties. Finish cushion and tie to chair post.

94

Hook and Loop Tabs

Hook and loop tape tabs make a cushion extremely easy to attach and remove, and because they are small and inconspicuous they blend in well with furniture.

The length of the tab depends on the size of the rung or post that the tab goes around. Measure accurately because the tabs must fit snugly. Tabs may be hand-stitched to existing cushions because they do not need to be stitched in a seam.

✂ Cutting Directions

Cut tabs just long enough to go around chair post and overlap by 1" to 1½" (2.5 to 3.8 cm), plus ½" (1.3 cm) for seam; twice the finished width, plus ½" (1.3 cm).

Cut hook and loop tape 1" to 1½" (2.5 to 3.8 cm) long for each tab.

How to Make Cushion Ties with Hook and Loop Tape

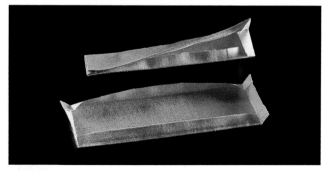

1) **Make** one tab for each corner. Press under ¼" (6 mm) on each edge of tab. Press tab in half lengthwise, wrong sides together. Edgestitch all four sides of tab.

2) **Cut** hook and loop tape for each tab. Separate hook and loop sides. Attach opposite sides of tape to opposite sides of tab. Stitch around all four sides of hook and loop tape.

3) **Stitch** pillow front to back. Before stuffing, pin center of tab to seam at cushion corners. Place all tabs in same direction; stitch and backstitch.

4) **Finish** cushion. Attach cushion to chair or bench by fastening hook and loop tabs around posts, overlapping ends to secure.

Tables

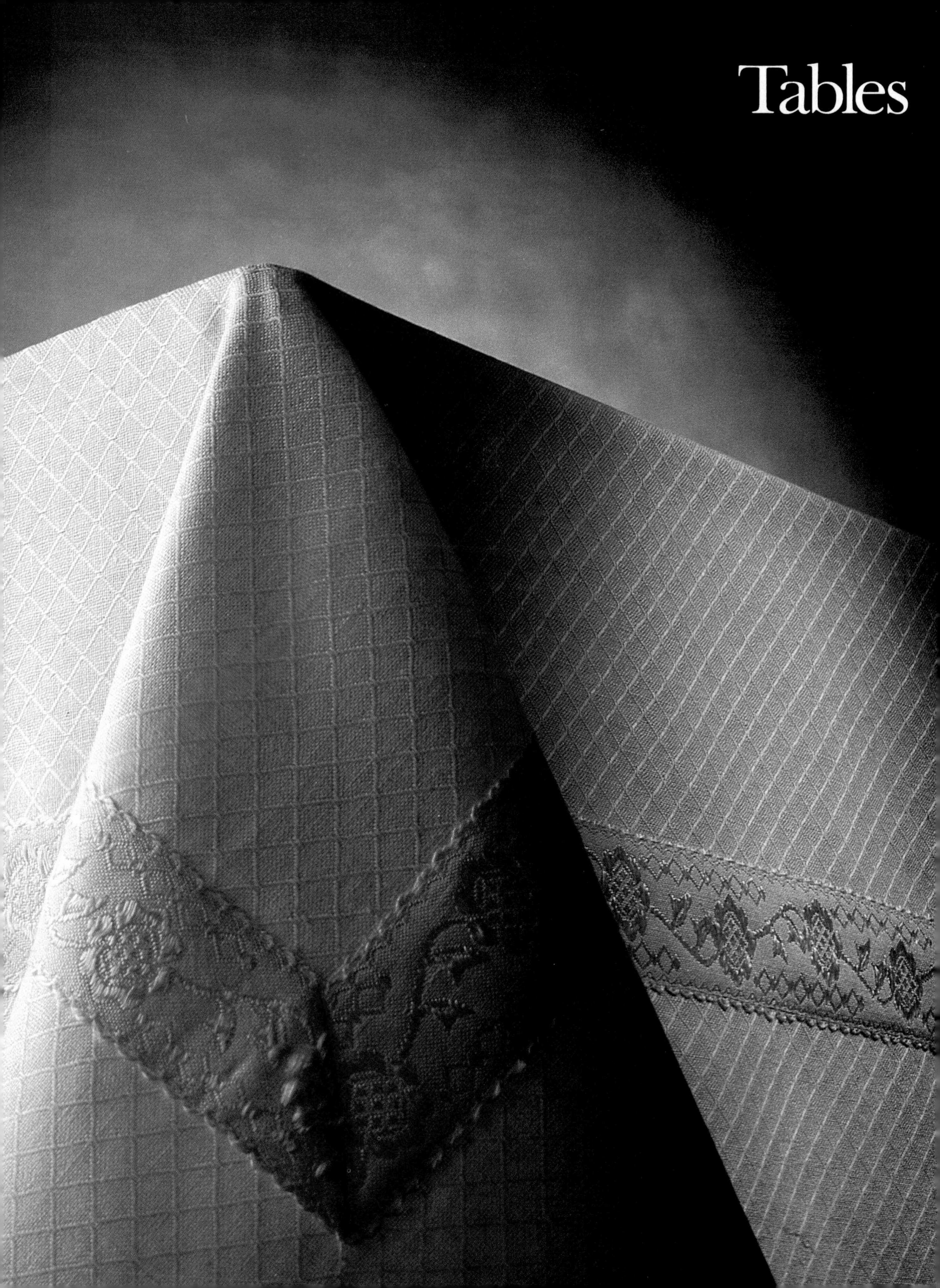

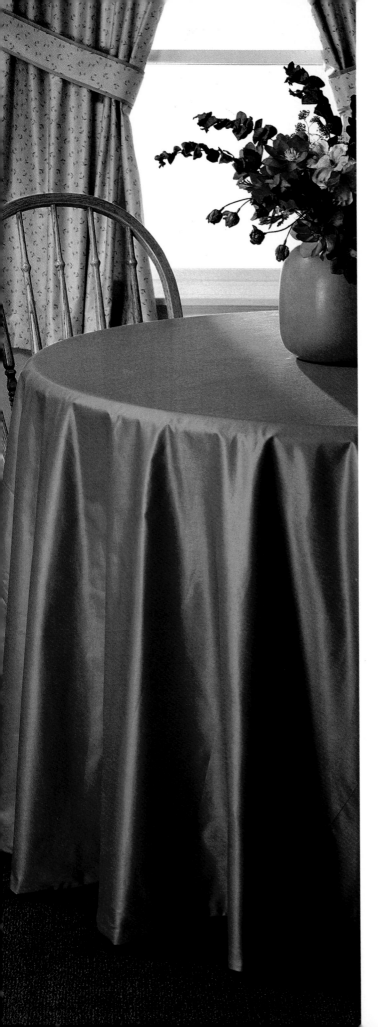

Tabletop Fashions

Customized tabletop fashions are a simple way to change the look of a room without spending too much time or money. These easy projects make good home sewing sense for several reasons.

Home-sewn table fashions, unlike purchased ones, are not limited to a small selection of standard sizes. Design a tablecloth yourself, and scale it to the exact size and shape of your table. Choose from an abundant supply of fabric colors, patterns and textures to complement the decor of your room.

Placemats, napkins and table runners are an excellent way to use up fabrics left over from other home sewing projects, and to color-coordinate these fashion accessories to your room at the same time. Small projects also give you an opportunity to experiment with finishing techniques you would be reluctant to try on larger projects.

Selecting Fabrics

When you design tabletop fashions, look for durable, stain-resistant fabrics that have been treated to repel soil and water. Permanent press fabrics offer easy care. Drape the fabric over your arm to see how it hangs.

Select decorator fabrics that are compatible with the tablecloth's use. For everyday use, lightweight cotton is appropriate; use a lightweight tablecloth with a table pad to protect fine wood tables. For an elegant look, use a sheer lace or eyelet tablecloth over a heavier cloth.

Quilted fabrics give tables a cozy look and provide protection. Protect tables, too, by lining the tablecloth or by placing firm, flat batting under it.

Small prints are easier to work with than large prints which may need matching. Avoid heavily napped fabrics or fabrics with difficult-to-match design motifs such as printed plaids or stripes, diagonals or one-way patterns.

Measuring the Table

The length of the tablecloth from the table's edge to the bottom of the cloth is the *drop*. Always include the drop length in your tablecloth measurements.

There are three common drop lengths: short, 10" to 12" (25.5 to 30.5 cm); mid-length, 16" to 24" (40.5 to 61 cm); and floor-length 28" to 29" (71 to 73.5 cm). Short cloths end at about chair seat height and are good tablecloths for everyday use. Mid-length cloths are more formal. Elegant floor-length coverings are used for buffet and decorator tables.

Round tablecloth. Measure the diameter of the table, then determine the drop length of the cloth. The size of the tablecloth is the diameter of the table plus twice the drop length plus 1" (2.5 cm) for a narrow hem allowance. A narrow hem is the easiest way to finish the curved edge of a round tablecloth.

Square tablecloth. Measure the width of the tabletop, then determine the drop length of the cloth. Add twice the drop length plus 1" (2.5 cm) for a narrow hem allowance or 2½" (6.3 cm) for a wide hem allowance.

Rectangular tablecloth. Measure the length and width of the tabletop, then determine the drop length of the cloth. The size of the finished tablecloth is the width of the tabletop plus twice the drop length, and the length of the tabletop plus twice the drop length. Add 1" (2.5 cm) for a narrow hem or 2½" (6.3 cm) for a wide hem.

Oval tablecloth. Measure the length and width of the tabletop, then determine the drop length of the cloth. Join fabric widths as necessary to make a rectangular cloth the length of the tabletop plus twice the drop length, and the width of the tabletop plus twice the drop length; add 1" (2.5 cm) to each dimension for a narrow hem allowance. Put a narrow hem in an oval tablecloth because it is the simplest way to finish the curved edge. Because oval tables vary in shape, mark the finished size with the fabric on the table. Place weights on the table to hold fabric in place, then use a hem marker or cardboard gauge to mark the drop length evenly.

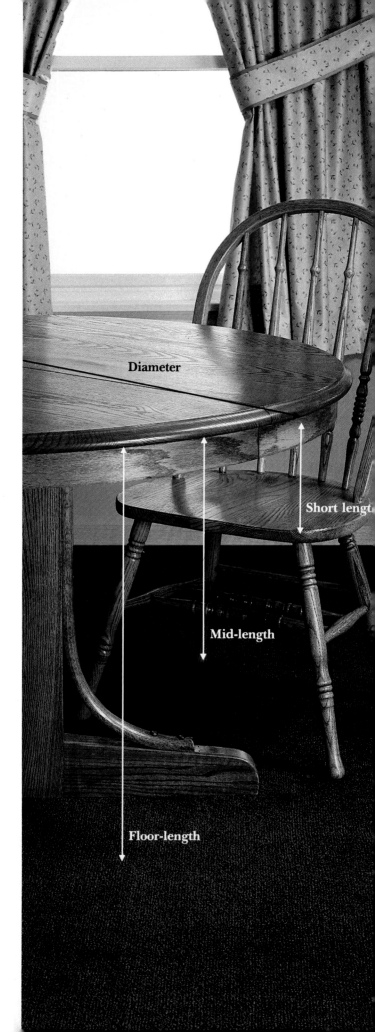

Diameter

Short length

Mid-length

Floor-length

Round Tablecloths

Because most tablecloths are wider than one fabric width, you must seam fabric widths together to make the cloth the width you need. Avoid a center seam by using a full fabric width in the center and stitching narrower side panels to it.

Use selvage edges in seams to eliminate seam finishing. If the selvage tends to pucker, clip it at regular intervals of about 1" (2.5 cm). If selvages are not used in seams, finish with French or overedge seams. Use plain seams for reversible tablecloths.

To determine the amount of fabric needed, divide the diameter of the tablecloth by the width of the fabric less 1" (2.5 cm). Count fractions as one width. This is the number of widths that must be seamed. Then multiply the number of panels by the diameter of the tablecloth, and divide this figure by 36" (100 cm) to find the total yards (meters).

✂ Cutting Directions
Cut center panel, length equal to diameter of finished tablecloth. Cut partial panels wide enough to form square equal to diameter of tablecloth plus hem. For reversible tablecloth, cut lining same size as decorator fabric.

How to Cut a Round Tablecloth

1) Join fabric panels together with ½" (1.3 cm) seams to form square. Fold square into fourths. Pin layers together to prevent slipping.

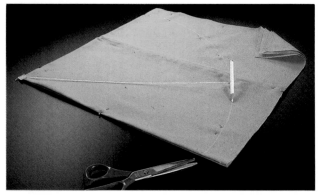

2) Measure a string the length of the radius of the cloth. Tie one end of string around a marking pencil; pin other end at center folded corner of cloth. Mark outer edge of circle, using string and pencil as compass. Cut on marked line; remove pins.

How to Sew Narrow & Flounced Hems

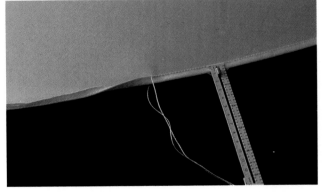

Narrow hem. Stitch around tablecloth ¼" (6 mm) from edge. Press under on stitching line. Press under ¼" (6 mm) again, easing fullness around curves. Edgestitch close to folded edge. Or, use narrow hemmer.

Flounced edge. Subtract two times the depth of the flounce from finished length of cloth and cut cloth accordingly. For ruffle, multiply *diameter* of cloth by 3½ and double measurement. Make ruffle and attach as for ruffled curtains (pages 38 and 39).

How to Sew a Corded Hem

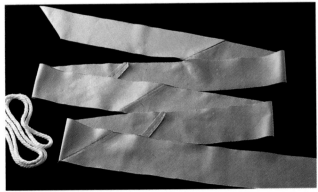

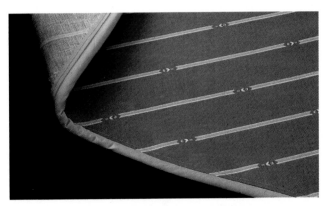

1) Multiply diameter of the cloth by 3½ to determine length of cording needed. Cut bias strips to cover cording (page 74).

2) Cover cording and attach to right side of cloth as for corded pillow (pages 74 and 75, steps 1 to 7). Zigzag seam and press to back of cloth. Topstitch ¼" (6 mm) from cording seam.

How to Sew a Reversible Round Tablecloth

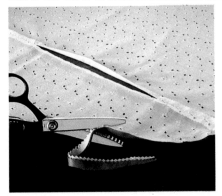

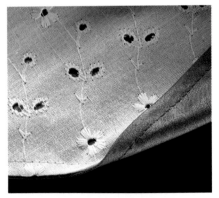

1) Join lining panels, leaving 12" (30.5 cm) opening in one seam for turning. Stitch lining and outer cloth together, wrong sides together, ½" (1.3 cm) from edge. Trim seam or clip curves.

2) Turn cloth right side out by pulling decorator fabric through opening in lining seam. Slipstitch opening closed.

3) Topstitch ¼" (6 mm) from edge. If lining is contrasting color, match upper thread to decorator fabric, bobbin thread to lining.

Square & Rectangular Tablecloths

Make tablecloths the desired width by joining fabric widths as necessary, using full widths in the center and partial widths on lengthwise edges. Use French or overedge seams, or use selvage edges to eliminate seam finishing.

Hems may be 1" or 2" (2.5 or 5 cm) wide, depending on the hemming technique you choose. Select a hem finish to complement the fabric's weight and texture. Mitering is the neatest way to square corners because it covers raw edges and eliminates bulk.

Determine the amount of fabric needed for the tablecloth by dividing the total width of the tablecloth by the width of your fabric, minus 1" (2.5 cm) for piecing seams. Multiply this figure, which is the number of panels needed, by the total length of the tablecloth. Divide this number by 36" (100 cm) to get the total yards (meters) required.

Wide and Narrow Hems

Wide hems. Press under ¼" (6 mm), then press under 1" or 2" (2.5 or 5 cm) hem on all sides.

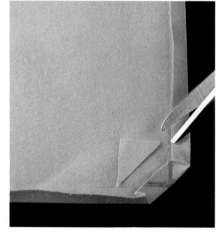

Mitered corners on narrow hems. Press under double-fold ¼" (6 mm) hem. Open out at corners. Trim corners diagonally. Bring hem edges together to form miter. Straight-stitch hem.

Mitered corners on wide hems. Miter corners as for double flange pillow (page 83, steps 2 to 7). Blindstitch or straight-stitch hem.

Quilted Table Covers

Quilting adds body to table coverings and provides additional protection for table surfaces. The thickness and slight puffiness of quilted table accessories also adds visual appeal. Use quilted fabrics for placemats, table runners and table mats.

Pre-quilted fabrics are available but quilting your own fabric provides the luxury of coordinating colors and prints, and the economy of making only the amount of quilted fabric needed for a project. The quilting guide foot with the attached guide bar make the channel-quilting process easy. Lengthen the stitch length and loosen the pressure for the most even quilting. Begin by stitching the center quilting row, and work toward the sides.

Use needle punched batting for tabletop fashions. This washable polyester batting will retain its shape and body when laundered.

How to Machine Quilt Fabric

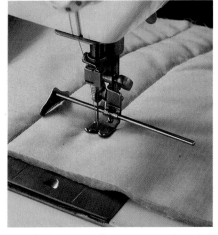

1) Cut fabric, batting and lining slightly larger than finished size of item. Place batting between wrong sides of fabric and lining. Pin or baste all three layers together.

2) Mark first quilting line in center of fabric with yardstick and washable marking pencil. If not using quilter bar, mark every quilting row equal distances apart.

3) Stitch center line. Determine the distance to next quilting line. Adjust quilter bar to follow the previous row of stitching as you stitch the next row.

Placemats, Table Runners & Table Mats

Placemats, table runners and table mats protect tabletops and add color and style to settings. Use them over tablecloths, or alone to show off the beauty of wood and glass tables. The sewing techniques for placemats, table runners and table mats are very similar.

Select fabric for mats and runners according to the general guidelines for choosing tablecloth fabrics. Fabric may be machine quilted using the procedure described on page 103.

Placemats can be lined, underlined with fusible interfacing, made of quilted fabric, or sewn double for extra body. Two common finished sizes of placemats are 18" × 12" (46 × 30.5 cm) and 16" × 14" (40.5 × 35.5 cm). Choose the best size for your table and place settings.

Table runners are usually 12" to 18" (30.5 to 46 cm) wide; make them wider if they will be used as placemats. Drop lengths vary from 8" to 12" (20.5 to 30.5 cm). Table runners may be cut either on the

Tips for Binding Placemat Edges

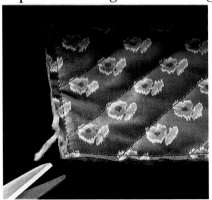

Quilted fabrics. Before applying binding, baste outer edges together, ¼" (6 mm) from edge. Trim batting from hem area to reduce bulk in bound edge.

Slipstitched edges. Open out bias tape. Pin along edge of mat, right sides together. Stitch on foldline. Turn tape to *back* of mat and slipstitch along edge.

Topstitched edges. Open out bias tape. Pin right side of tape to *wrong* side of mat. Stitch on foldline. Turn tape to *front* of mat and topstitch.

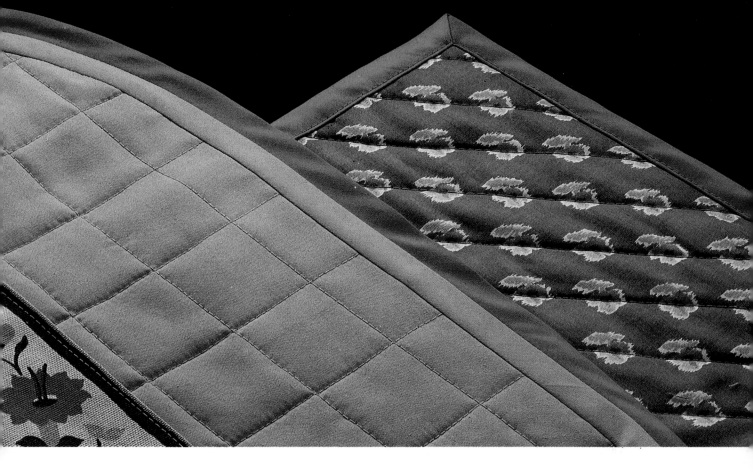

lengthwise or crosswise grain of the fabric, but less piecing of fabric is required if they are cut on lengthwise grain.

Table runners may be lighter weight than placemats. If they are used only as decoration over a tablecloth, finish them with hemmed edges. When table runners will also be used as placemats, machine quilt or pad them to protect the table surface; finish the edges with bias binding which may be slipstitched or topstitched in place.

Table mats protect a table's surface without hiding the legs or base. Cut and sew a mat to the exact size of the tabletop and finish it using an appropriate bound edge finish.

Reduce bulk along quilted edges of tabletop projects by binding them with bias tape. Apply binding as described below, or use the binder attachment on your machine. Edges of tabletop projects may also be banded, a finishing technique similar to binding which gives a wider decorative edge.

Square mats. Fold bias tape binding over one side of mat and pin. Topstitch to corner. Pin bias tape to next side, turning under diagonally at corner to form miter. Begin stitching at miter.

Oval mats. Shape corners of rectangular mat using a dinner plate as a guide. Before applying bias tape, preshape tape to curves with a steam iron.

Finishing ends. Cut binding 1" (2.5 cm) beyond end. Turn under ½" (1.3 cm) and finish stitching to end of tape. Slipstitch if necessary.

Banded Placemats

Wide banding makes an impressive framed placemat. The mitered corners require careful attention; check each one before proceeding to the next.

✂ Cutting Directions

Cut placemat center, allowing ½" (1.3 cm) extra for seam. To make mat reversible, cut two fabric centers. Stitch wrong sides of centers together a scant ¼" (6 mm) from the edge.

Cut banding twice the desired finished width plus ½" (1.3 cm) for seams. Cut banding long enough to go around edge of mat; add twice the finished width of banding for each corner to allow for mitering.

How to Sew Banded Placemats with Mitered Corners

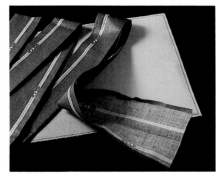

1) Press banding in half lengthwise, wrong sides together. Open out banding. Press raw edges under ¼" (6 mm).

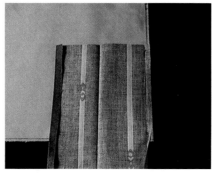

2) Open one folded edge. Beginning at center of one side, pin right sides of mat and banding together. Stitch on foldline, ending ¼" (6 mm) from corner; backstitch.

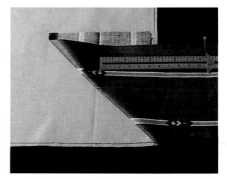

3) Fold banding away from mat diagonally. Measure from center of banding to a distance twice the width of the finished banding; mark with a pin or snip.

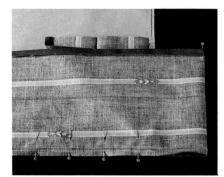

4) Fold banding back from mark. Pin lower fold of banding to next edge. Stitch outer fold ¼" (6 mm) from edge, ending ¼" (6 mm) from corner. Repeat at each corner.

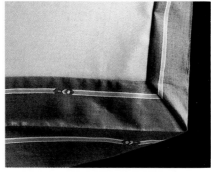

5) Open out banding and form miter on right side of mat at each corner. Fold banding to wrong side of mat on center foldline.

6) Pin folded edge of banding to stitching line on back of the mat. Slipstitch mitered corners and edges of banding in place.

Trimmed Placemats

A band of trimming may be stitched directly on the edge of a finished placemat. Use purchased grosgrain ribbon, embroidered ribbon or woven ribbon trimmings. Trimmings may also be cut from coordinating fabrics.

✂ Cutting Directions

Cut placemat 1" (2.5 cm) larger than desired finished size. Press ½" (1.3 cm) to right side on all edges.

Cut trimming strip long enough to go around edge of placemat plus 1" (2.5 cm). If making your own trimming, allow ¼" (6 mm) on each side for finishing; press under ¼" (6 mm) on long ends.

How to Sew Placemats with Mitered Ribbon Trimming

1) Pin trimming to one edge of placemat. Edgestitch outer edge starting from center on one side of placemat to a corner. Pull threads to inside and tie.

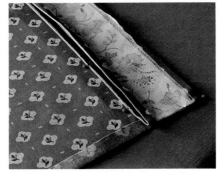

2) Fold trimming straight back on itself so fold is even with lower edge of placemat. Pin at fold.

3) Fold trimming down along lower edge, creating a diagonal fold at the corner. Press fold.

4) Lift up trimming at corner and stitch on the diagonal press line through all thicknesses. Trim stitched fold to ¼" (6 mm) to reduce bulk.

5) Fold trimming back along lower edge and stitch next side. Repeat for each corner.

6) Pull threads to wrong side at corner and tie. Stitch along inner edge of trimming.

Six Ways to Make and Hem Napkins

Satin stitch. Turn under ½"
(1.3 cm) on all sides. Miter corners
(page 102). Edgestitch raw edge to
use as guide. Set zigzag at widest
buttonhole setting or closely spaced
zigzag (satin stitch). Stitch from
right side over straight stitch.

Zigzag overedge. Trim loose
threads from napkin edges. Satin
stitch over raw edge. This stitch
will draw fabric into a narrow
edge. Use overedge foot to
maintain zigzag width.

Decorative stitch. Press under ¼"
(6 mm) and stitch. From right side,
stitch with a pattern stitch, using
straight stitch as guide line.
Blanket stitch (shown above) gives
a hemstitched look.

Napkins

Coordinating napkins are the finishing touch to your tabletop fashions. Standard finished napkins are 14" (35.5 cm) or 17" (43 cm) square.

Napkin hems can be inconspicuous or decorative. Experiment with some of the decorative stitches on your sewing machine. These six hemming techniques shown here can also be used on tablecloths and placemats.

✂ Cutting Directions

Cut napkins 1" (2.5 cm) larger than finished size. One yard (meter) of 36" (91.5 cm) wide fabric yields four 17" (43 cm) napkins. A piece of fabric 45" (115 cm) square yields nine 14" (35.5 cm) napkins.

Quick narrow hem. Press under double-fold ¼" (6 mm) hem on opposite sides of all napkins. Edgestitch from one napkin to the next using continuous stitching. Repeat for remaining sides.

Double-fold hem. Turn under ¼" (6 mm) on all edges and press. Turn under another ¼" (6 mm) and edgestitch close to folded edge. Miter corners as directed for narrow hems (page 102).

Fringe. Cut napkins on a pulled thread to straighten edges. Stitch ½" (1.3 cm) from raw edges with short straight stitches or narrow, closely spaced zigzag. Pull out threads up to the stitching line.

Beds

Bed Fashions

Decorate the bedroom with custom-made bed fashions such as comforters, comforter covers, pillow shams and dust ruffles.

Projects for the bed can be frilly or tailored to suit the bedroom's decor. Chintzes, polished cottons and sateens are good general-purpose choices for most bed coverings. Sheets are another practical fabric choice; their width makes seaming unnecessary on comforters and covers.

Permanent press fabrics with soil-resistant finishes are advisable in a child's room. Also think about how often the bed covering might be cleaned, and select fabrics that will launder well without fading.

Comforters are a useful alternative to bedspreads. Make them reversible to change their look, and fill them with polyester batting as flat or as puffy as you wish. Decorator fabrics used for comforters should be pieced together with a full fabric width in the center of the comforter and partial width on each side.

Comforter covers, also known as *duvet covers,* are removable for easy care. They protect new comforters, salvage worn ones, quickly change a comforter's look, and eliminate the need for a top sheet and blanket on the bed.

Pillow shams are removable, decorative pillow covers. Make pillow shams plain or flanged, ruffled or trimmed, in matching or contrasting fabrics to complement the comforter and dust ruffle. Traditional pillowcases may also be trimmed with ruffles and used as pillow shams.

Dust ruffles, or bed skirts, are used with comforters. They may be gathered, pleated or flat. Make them in one piece for beds that do not have a footboard or with slits at the corners to fit over a bed frame. Attach dust ruffles to a fitted sheet placed over the boxspring or to a muslin *deck,* a piece of fabric which fits between the mattress and the boxspring.

Fabrics for dust ruffles, although not often handled, should be considered for their weight and draping quality, as well as suitablilty for the style of the dust ruffle or bed skirt.

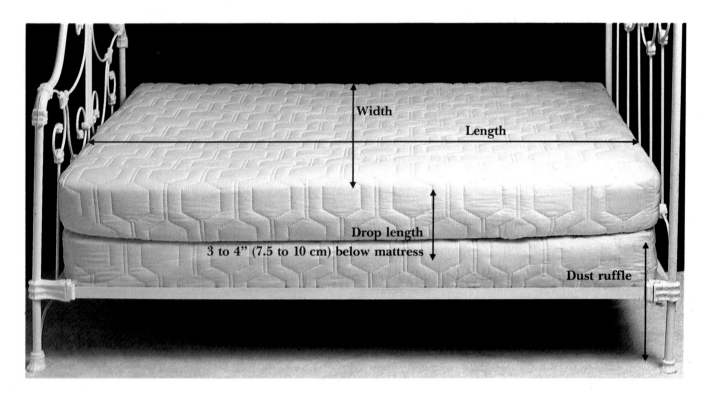

Measuring the Bed

Measure accurately to make comforters and dust ruffles that fit beds perfectly.

Comforters reach 3" to 4" (7.5 to 10 cm) below the mattress line. They have a *drop length* (the distance from the upper edge of the mattress to the bottom of the comforter) of 9" to 12" (23 to 30.5 cm), depending on the depth of the mattress. Determine drop length by measuring from the top of the mattress to the top of the boxspring, then adding to that figure the amount of overlap desired. Take into account fabric stiffness which may cause the comforter to stand away from the side of the bed.

To determine finished comforter size, measure from side to side across the top of the mattress for width, and from the head to the foot of the bed for length. Add the desired drop length to the bed's length, and

twice the drop length to the bed's width for finished measurements.

Batting for comforters is available in standard widths for standard sized beds; select the proper size for your comforter.

For the finished ruffle length, measure from the top of the boxspring to the floor; for the deck, measure the width and length of the boxspring.

Pillow sizes are 20" × 26" (51 × 66 cm) standard; 20" × 30" (51 × 76 cm) queen; and 20" × 40" (51 × 102 cm) king. Pillow puffiness varies, however, so make the best fitting shams by measuring the width and length of the pillow with a tape measure across the center of the pillow. Ruffled shams made from lightweight fabrics will droop around the edges if they are cut too large.

Comforter

Comforters have the look of quilts but do not require time-consuming and intricate hand-quilting. They should reach just below the mattress line and be used with dust ruffles or bed skirts.

Comforters are made from three layers: a backing or lining, a bonded polyester fiberfill for warmth and body, and a top layer of decorator fabric.

Because the comforter's bulk makes machine-quilting difficult to manage, it should be hand-tufted. Tufting, or hand-tied yarn, holds the layers together and emphasizes the comforter's appealing puffiness. Place tufts 6" to 10" (15 to 25.5 cm) apart; the fabric's design may dictate their placement.

✂ Cutting Directions

Cut and seam fabric for comforter top equal to finished size. Cut lining 8" (20.5 cm) larger than finished size for self-binding edge. *Or* cut lining same as top; finish edge with wide bias binding strips as for quilted placemats (pages 104 and 105).

YOU WILL NEED

Decorator fabric for comforter.

Lining for comforter.

Bonded polyester batting, proper size for bed width and cut to finished size of comforter.

Yarn, pearl cotton or embroidery floss for tufting, washable if comforter will be laundered.

How to Sew and Tuft a Comforter

1) Place lining face down on flat surface. Leaving 4" (10 cm) border, place batting on lining, then decorator fabric, right side up, edges even with batting.

2) Pin three layers together. Hand-baste layers together with long stitches in parallel rows 8" to 10" (20.5 to 25.5 cm) apart, so layers do not slip.

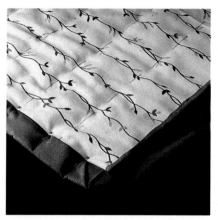

3) Fold lining to edge of batting, then fold again over front of comforter to form 2" (5 cm) border. Pin in place. Miter corners as for square mats (page 106). Slipstitch binding to comforter along folded edge.

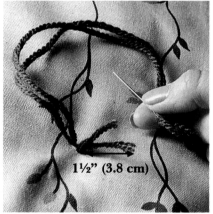

1½" (3.8 cm)

4) Mark positions for tufts. Thread a large needle with double strand of yarn. Working from right side of comforter, make a ¼" (6 mm) stitch through all layers. Leave 1½" (3.8 cm) tail of yarn.

5) Hold all four strands of yarn in one hand, close to comforter. Bring needle behind four strands and over two strands to form loop.

6) Draw needle through loop. Pull ends to secure knot. Clip ends of yarn to ¾" (2 cm).

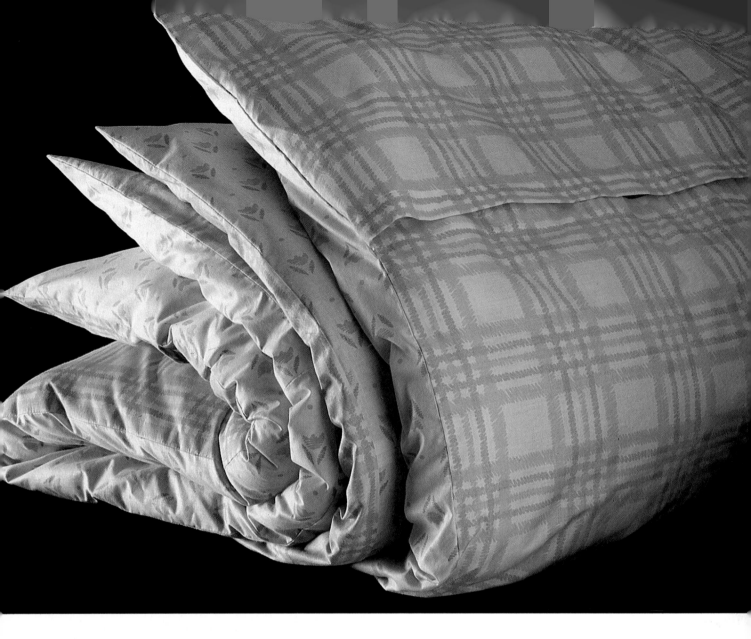

Comforter Cover

Change the look of a bed with a covered comforter. It takes the place of a top sheet and blanket, and the comforter's removable cover makes laundering easy. Sew your own comforter, or use a purchased down or polyester one.

Choose a washable, lightweight, firmly woven fabric for the cover. Sheets are good fabric choices because they do not require piecing. Seam narrower decorator fabrics together by using a full fabric width in the center of the cover, with partial widths along the sides.

Leave a 36" (91.5 cm) opening in the back of the cover for inserting the comforter. Place the opening about 16" (40.5 cm) from the lower edge on the inside of the cover so it will not show at the ends. Use an overlap, snap tape, hook and loop tape, a zipper or buttons for closure.

✂ Cutting Directions

Cut the front of the cover 1" (2.5 cm) larger than the comforter. Cut the back according to the closure method you choose. For overlap or button closures, cut the back 5½" (14 cm) longer. For a snap tape, hook and loop or zipper closure, cut the back 1½" (3.8 cm) longer than the front.

Cut four small fabric strips for tabs, each about 2" (5 cm) square.

YOU WILL NEED

Decorator fabric or sheets for cover, and small amount of extra fabric for tabs.

Snap tape, hook and loop tape, zipper or buttons.

Gripper snaps to hold comforter in place.

How to Sew a Comforter Cover

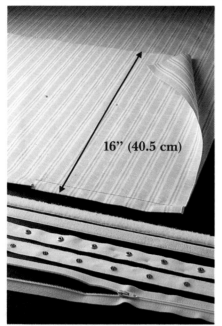

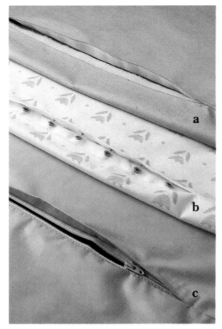

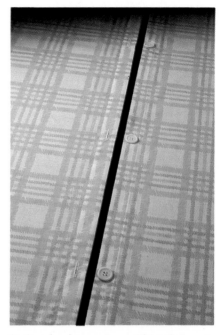

1) Press under 16" (40.5 cm) across bottom of back, right sides together. If using tapes or zipper, snip fold to mark ends of closure. Stitch ¾" (2 cm) seam on fold; backstitch at snips and bastestitch across area where closure will be inserted. Cut on fold; press seam open.

2) Insert hook and loop tape **(a)**, snap tape **(b)** or zipper **(c)** according to instructions for pillow closures (pages 89 and 90). Omit step 3 if using one of the closures above. For a button closure continue with step 3.

3) Cut back apart on 16" (40.5 cm) fold line for button closure. Press under ¼" (6 mm) then 1" (2.5 cm) hem on each edge; edgestitch. On hem of narrow piece, make buttonholes 10" to 12" (25.5 to 30.5 cm) apart; attach buttons opposite buttonholes.

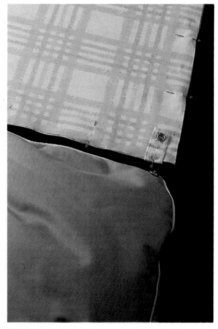

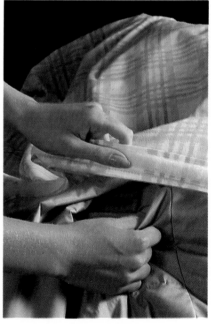

4) Pin cover front to cover back, right sides together. For button closure, pin the narrow piece first, lapping longer piece over it.

5) Make tabs (page 95, step 1). Attach socket side of snaps to tabs, and ball sides to corners of the comforter. Pin a tab at each corner of the cover, edges even.

6) Stitch front and back of cover together with ½" (1.3 cm) seam. Diagonally trim bulk from corners. Turn cover right side out. Insert comforter; snap cover to comforter at corners.

Pillow Shams

Pillow shams are attractive, loose-fitting pillow covers that can be made to coordinate with a comforter or comforter cover. They can be plain, ruffled or trimmed with a flange or banding.

A sham has an overlap or flap pocket on the back to make it easy to slip a pillow into it. The easiest sham to make is cut in one piece with the ends turned under and hemmed so that the pocket is part of the fold. To add a ruffle or coordinating flange, cut the front, back and pocket flap pieces separately so that there will be a seam completely around the pillow. French seams are used to cover all raw edges.

✂ Cutting Directions

For one-piece sham, cut fabric same width as pillow plus 1" (2.5 cm); length equal to two times the length of pillow plus 10" (25.5 cm).

For ruffled sham, cut front and back 1" (2.5 cm) larger than pillow. Cut pocket flap 10" (25.5 cm) wide, length equal to width of pillow plus 1" (2.5 cm). Cut ruffle two times desired width plus 1" (2.5 cm), and length equal to two times the distance around pillow.

For sham with flange, cut front, back and pocket 4" (10 cm) larger than ruffled sham (above). Cut banding or trimming desired width and long enough to go around entire pillow.

For ruffled pillow case sham, cut fabric same width as pillow plus 1" (2.5 cm); length equal to two times the length of pillow plus 1" (2.5 cm). Cut ruffle two times desired width plus 1" (2.5 cm), and length four times width of pillow. Cut facing strip 3" (7.5 cm) wide; length equal to two times the width of pillow plus ½" (1.3 cm).

How to Sew a One-piece Sham

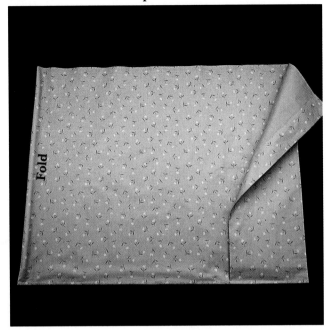

1) Stitch double-fold ¼" (6 mm) hem at one short end. Turn under ½" (1.3 cm) then 2" (5 cm) at the other end. For pocket flap, press under 7½" (19.3 cm) on end with wider hem. Fold sham crosswise, wrong sides together so that narrow hemmed edge is on pressed fold. Fold pocket over hemmed edge.

2) Stitch ¼" (6 mm) seam on two long sides. Trim seams to ⅛" (3 mm). Turn sham wrong side out. Press. Stitch ¼" (6 mm) French seam to finish inside of sham. Turn sham right side out. Insert pillow, overlapping pocket flap at end.

How to Sew a Ruffled Sham

1) Stitch ½" (1.3 cm) hem on one short end of sham back. Turn under ½" (1.3 cm), then 2" (5 cm) hem on one long edge of pocket flap. Edgestitch. Prepare ruffle as for ruffled pillow (page 80 and 81, steps 1 to 4). Attach ruffle to right side of sham front, stitching ½" (1.3 cm) from edge.

2) Pin unfinished edge of flap to one end of front, right sides together, with ruffle in seam between two layers. Pin front to back with hemmed edge of back overlapping hem of flap. Stitch ½" (1.3 cm) seam around sham. Trim corners. Turn right side out and insert pillow.

How to Sew a Sham with Flange

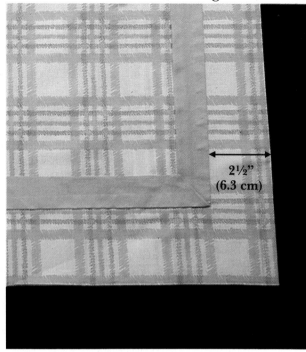

1) Pin ribbon banding to front of pillow sham 2½" (6.3 cm) from edge. Sew banding and miter corners, as for placemats with mitered ribbon trimming, (page 107, steps 1 to 6).

2) Make sham following instructions for ruffled sham, (page 119), omitting ruffle. Turn sham right side out and topstitch along edge of trimming, 2" (5 cm) from edge of sham. Insert pillow.

How to Sew a Ruffled Pillowcase Sham

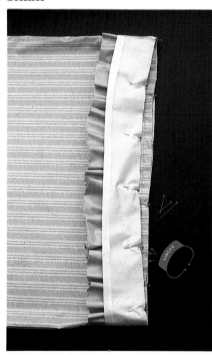

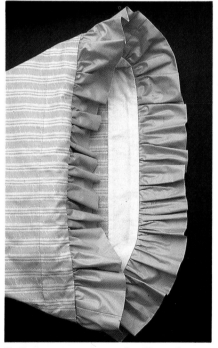

1) Fold one-piece sham crosswise, wrong sides together; stitch French seams. Prepare ruffle as directed, (pages 80 and 81, steps 1 to 4). Turn sham right side out; bastestitch ruffle to right side of open end.

2) Press under ½" (1.3 cm) on one long side of facing. Join short ends of strip. Pin right side of facing strip to right side of pillow sham with ruffle between two fabric layers. Stitch ½" (1.3 cm) seam.

3) Press seam toward pillow sham. Edgestitch or slipstitch along pressed fold of facing. Facing strip is shown in contrasting color to make it more visible.

Dust Ruffles & Bed Skirts

Dust ruffles can be made to color-coordinate with the comforter or quilt. By making your own dust ruffle, you can get a precise ruffle depth with nonstandard bed heights.

Choose a fabric according to the style of the finished ruffle. Sheers such as eyelet and dotted Swiss need very full gathering to look their best; light to mediumweight fabrics such as chintz or cotton blends also gather well. Sailcloth and other heavyweight materials are good choices for pleated or tailored skirts.

Attach the ruffle to a fitted bed sheet or to a muslin deck, seamed and cut to the size of the box spring. To fit the ruffle over a bed frame, cut the fabric at the corners into three separate ruffle pieces, adding 4" (10 cm) at each corner to allow for 2" (5 cm) double-fold hems. In calculating the amount of fabric needed for the ruffle, remember that they are only finished along three sides.

Gathered dust ruffles require two to four times fullness, depending on the fabric's weight. A ruffler attachment saves time on such large projects.

Pleated bed skirts have deep, evenly spaced box pleats about 12" (30.5 cm) apart. Space them carefully across the foot of the bed; uneven spacing at the head of the bed can be hidden by end tables.

To determine spacing and the number of pleats, divide the width of the bed by a number which will yield a whole number: on a single bed 39" (99 cm) divided by 3 gives 13" (33 cm) spacing. Use that spacing to figure the number of pleats along both sides of the bed.

To get the total yardage, multiply the total number of pleats by the desired pleat depth: a 6" (15 cm) pleat requires 12" (30.5 cm) additional fabric, 3" (7.5 cm) on each side of the pleat, 6" (15 cm) across the back. Add this figure to the distance around three sides of the bed, allowing extra for seams.

✂ Cutting Directions

Cut fabric with length according to style of ruffle and size of mattress; width equal to distance from top of box spring to floor plus 4" (10 cm) for seam and hem.

If making deck, cut and seam muslin the size of the top of box spring.

YOU WILL NEED

Decorator fabric for dust ruffle or bed skirt.

Fitted sheet, or muslin for deck.

How to Sew a Gathered Dust Ruffle with Open Corners

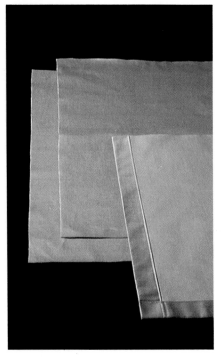

1) Stitch double-fold 1" (2.5 cm) hem along bottom of the three ruffle sections, then turn under and stitch 1" (2.5 cm) double-fold hem on both ends of each of the sections.

2) Gather 1" (2.5 cm) from upper edge with ruffler attachment **(a)**, two-string shirring tape **(b)**, two rows bastestitching **(c)**, or zigzag over cord **(d)**.

3) Place fitted sheet on box spring. On the sheet, mark upper edge of box spring. Then mark every 12" (30.5 cm) along this line. Mark upper edge of ruffle every 24" (61 cm) for double fullness, every 36" (91.5 cm) for triple fullness.

How to Sew a Pleated Bed Skirt

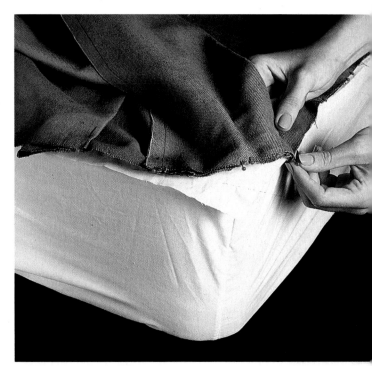

1) Hem skirt as in step 1 above, seaming sections for desired length. Measure and mark pleats as determined, positioning seams to fall inside pleats.

2) Place muslin deck on box spring. Beginning with a pleat at center of foot of bed, pin pleats to deck. Adjust pleats to fall at each corner.

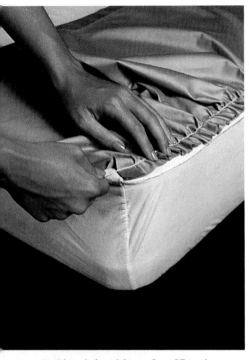

4) Pin right sides of ruffle pieces along three sides of sheet, raw edges on marked line and hems overlapping at corners. Match markings on ruffles to markings on sheet. Pull up gathering cord to fit.

5) Remove sheet from box spring, keeping ruffle pinned in place. Stitch on gathering line, 1" (2.5 cm) from raw edge of ruffle.

6) Turn ruffle down over lower edge of sheet. Topstitch ½" (1.3 cm) from seam, stitching through ruffle and sheet.

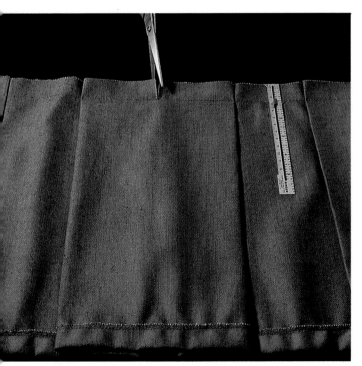

3) Remove skirt from deck. Machine-baste pleats in place 1" (2.5 cm) from raw edge. Clip corner pleats to stitching line so they will spread at corners.

4) Pin right side of skirt to deck, raw edges even. Stitch 1" (2.5 cm) from raw edges.

Index